EnglishSmart in 90 Days 6

Margaret Ramsay

Copyright © 2006 **Popular Book Company (Canada) Limited**

Printed in China

Contents

EnglishSmart in 90 Days

GRADE 6

Get up!

"Get up!" Do these words startle you from a deep sleep and signal how you begin your day? Do you just know that it is not the first time your Mom or Dad has yelled it that morning? You are suffering! Did you realize that what you are suffering from is "sleep deprivation"?

Pre-teens and adolescents need between eight and nine hours of sleep a night. If you do not get enough sleep one night, it is not as easy as you think to just catch up by sleeping in on Saturday. You build up a sleep debt and then you will show symptoms of sleep deprivation. You may not recognize the symptoms, but when you do not get enough sleep, you get irritated more easily. You have no patience. Everything you are asked to do takes extra effort. You feel sluggish. You just do not feel like walking to school. You want to get a ride instead.

The body needs sleep to refuel the brain for the next day. Humans have biological cycles. Bright light wakes you up and darkness helps you sleep. However, in this technological age, you can turn on bright lights at night and video games can stimulate you to ignore the normal cycles of the body. But, staying up late and playing games mean that eventually you will need to catch up.

Scientists divide sleep into five phases. For a true rest, our bodies should have cycles consisting of light sleep (phases one and two), deep sleep (phases three and four), and rapid eye movement, or REM, sleep (phase five). Deep sleep and REM sleep are the most important types of sleep. Deep sleep releases the growth hormone in children; REM sleep is when we dream. If we are woken too frequently or too soon, our bodies do not go into deep sleep and REM sleep.

If you do not get enough sleep, you are probably being woken from your deep sleep or REM sleep before having a chance to go into another phase of light sleep. That is why you might need several alarm clocks placed in random spots about your room and the screeching of your parents' voices to wake you up. Studies are also finding that adolescents are sleepiest between eight and nine in the morning!

A. Answer the following questions.

1. How many hours of sleep does a pre-teen need each night?

   _____

2. What are REMs?

   _____

3. Which phases are the most important types of sleep?

   _____

4. Can you infer from the passage what the word "deprivation" means? Write the meaning in your own words.

   _____

5. Why might someone need more than one alarm clock in order to wake up?

   _____

B. Complete the chart to practise the following irregular verbs.

	Present Tense	Past Tense	Past Participle
1.	wake		woken
2.	do		
3.	has	had	
4.	choose		chosen
5.	ride		ridden
6.	pay		paid
7.	forget		forgotten
8.	hide	hid	

Grammar Overview (1)

Grammar explains the role each type of word plays in a phrase or a sentence. We refer to the various word types as "**parts of speech**". There are eight parts of speech in English.

Noun: to name a person, a place, an object, an idea, or a feeling

A. Underline the nouns in the following sentences.

1. The restaurant serves Italian food.

2. Beauty is in the eye of the beholder.

3. The house was destroyed in the storm.

4. The teacher wrote a poem about friendship.

5. Where can you find a better place than this?

6. In the end, she was left with a sense of emptiness.

Pronoun: to stand in for a noun

B. Complete the paragraph about Ted with pronouns.

"1. _____ on earth is the gossip about?" wondered Ted. At first, 2. _____ thought that 3. _____ was the one his neighbours were talking about but soon realized that 4. _____ weren't talking about 5. _____ .

6. _____ was just being too sensitive and had almost made a fool of 7. _____ . Luckily, Ted's sister did not know about 8. _____ or 9. _____ would tell 10. _____ parents.

Verb: to describe an action or a state of being

C. Circle the verbs in the following paragraph.

The fox has excellent speed and can reach up to 50 km per hour. This speed, coupled with its cunning nature, has made the fox the traditional prey of the English foxhunt. Foxes often retrace their steps to throw off the scent of the pursuing hounds. They then hide in trees as the hounds and hunters speed past. Although foxes generally stay clear of humans, it is advisable not to approach them.

Adjective: to describe a noun or a pronoun

D. Complete the following paragraph about hockey with suitable adjectives.

> British   difficult   amateur   frozen   national   silver   frigid

It is 1._____ to argue that hockey is not the 2._____ passion of Canadians. Canada, with its 3._____ winter weather, is suitable for playing hockey. As early as 1870, 4._____ soldiers stationed in Halifax started playing hockey games on 5._____ ponds around the city. In 1892 Lord Stanley, the Governor-General of Canada, donated a 6._____ bowl to be awarded to the best 7._____ team. That was the origin of the Stanley Cup.

Video Games

"An aircraft circles over a crisis zone. War. Drought. People are hungry. This is the virtual world of the Food Force video game…"

"Play the Food Force game, learn about food aid, and help WFP work towards a world without hunger…"

These words introduce you to an exciting Website that teaches you about world hunger.

Food Force is an educational game developed by the United Nations's World Food Program. The purpose of the game is to help raise awareness that there are people starving all around the world. In this video game you control the World Food Program's missions to send food to nations in need. You are to send food to an imaginary country called Sheylan. You will find this game at www.food-force.com.

There are six missions in this game. You are the pilot, and you fly a helicopter around the country to find and count the number of hungry people. Second, you must plan a balanced diet for the people. You are given only a very small budget. Once you have located the people and planned the diet, you must plan the food drops from the aircraft to the people in need.

The challenge comes in planning the exact timing to the millisecond and dropping the food packages, taking into account the wind direction.

During the fourth mission, you must locate and order food from around the world. It is your responsibility to keep costs down so that you have enough money for the flights and fuel. Next you have to ship the food by truck into Sheylan. Just like in real life, your tires will keep blowing out on the unpaved roads and rough terrain of the forests and countryside.

Your final challenge is to help the small community rebuild and become independent.

A. The system the UN uses to provide food for hungry people in the world involves many steps. List the steps described in the game.

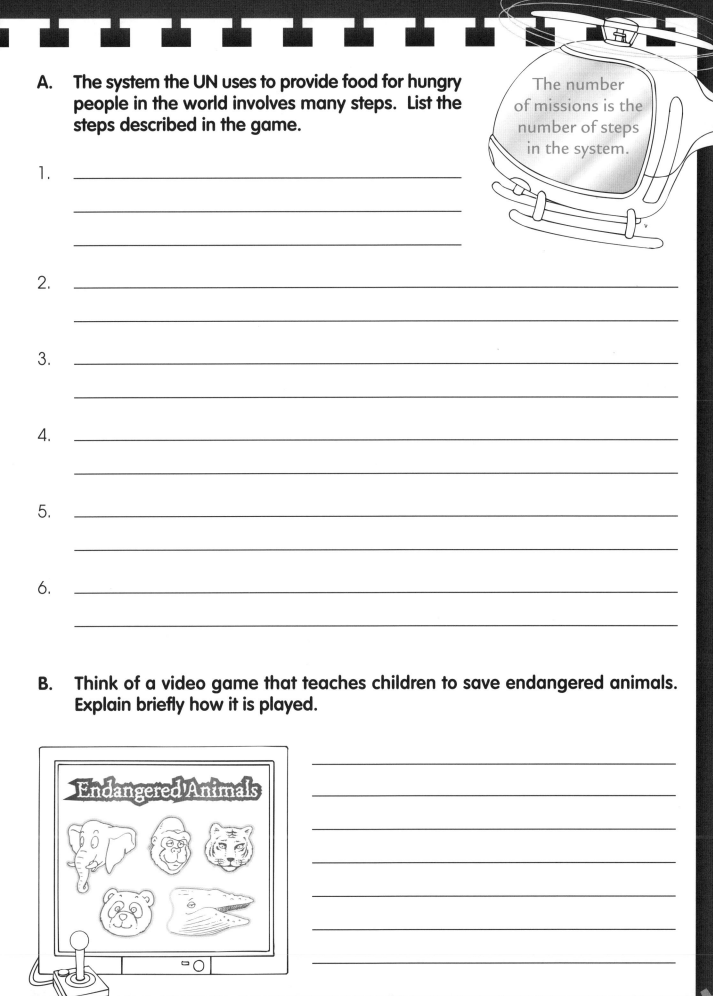

The number of missions is the number of steps in the system.

1. _____

   _____

   _____

2. _____

   _____

3. _____

   _____

4. _____

   _____

5. _____

   _____

6. _____

   _____

B. Think of a video game that teaches children to save endangered animals. Explain briefly how it is played.

Endangered Animals

_____

_____

_____

_____

_____

_____

_____

Day
4

Grammar Overview (2)

The other four parts of speech are: adverb, preposition, conjunction, and interjection.

Adverb: to modify the meaning of a verb, an adjective, or another adverb
Preposition: to express the relationship between words
Conjunction: to join words or phrases together
Interjection: to express emotion or excitement

A.   Add adverbs to the following sentences. Use "∧" to show where they should be put.

rather
knowingly
exceptionally
cautiously
almost

1.   That performance was good.

2.   It has been a year since we last saw him.

3.   He was not good at that and did it oddly.

4.   The slope was steep and they had to go down.

5.   He nodded and started figuring out how to settle the matter.

B.   Add prepositions to the following paragraph about J.K. Rowling.

Joanne Kathleen Rowling, author 1._____ the immensely popular Harry Potter series, went 2._____ ordinary existence 3._____ stardom virtually overnight. The fame bestowed 4._____ her was 5._____ her wildest dreams. As a single parent 6._____ little money, Joanne often headed 7._____ a café 8._____ write 9._____ the wizard and "Muggle" worlds.

C. Complete the following sentences with suitable conjunctions.

1. They like the bungalow _____ it is rather old _____ plain.

2. They were all surprised _____ they never expected me to win.

3. You can't go _____ you finish the work before noon.

4. He declined our offer _____ promised to help us out on weekends.

5. They became impatient _____ time was running out.

6. We will have a game of hockey _____ we have time.

7. You can have this one _____ that one _____ not both.

D. Add a suitable interjection to each of the following sentences.

Hurray	Yuck	Wow	Oops
Oh no	Great	Hey	Look out

1. _____ ! That's not the way to do it.

2. _____ ! That's the longest homerun I've seen.

3. _____ ! Let's start right away.

4. _____ ! I didn't realize it was the teacher; I thought it was Sam.

5. _____ ! Our team won again.

6. _____ ! A truck is coming right at you.

7. _____ ! It tastes awful.

8. _____ ! I dropped the vase.

Watch Where You Are Walking

Imagine your parents have just told you that you need to earn your TV-viewing time by being active. You need to play a soccer game, walk to school, jump rope at recess, play outside, visit a friend and walk while you talk. Haven't had enough exercise? No TV for you!

The day is not so far away. A British design graduate named Gillian Swan has designed the prototype of a product for parents to limit the number of hours a child watches TV. The device is an insole to put in the child's shoe. It has a pedometer, which is a counter to measure the number of steps a person takes in a day.

There is another sensor in the insole which then transmits the number of steps to a base station connected to the TV. You earn your TV-viewing time by stepping over 12 000 times if you are a girl and 15 000 if you are a boy. Swan designed the device to teach kids about healthy lifestyle choices. According to Dr. Glenn Berall, a member of the Healthy Active Living Committee of the Canadian Pediatric Society and Chief of Pediatrics at North York General Hospital, one in three Canadian children is overweight.

Swan hopes that the invention will encourage children to ask for time to exercise rather than extra time to watch TV. She predicts that children will find themselves in a situation where they will not be able to watch as much TV as they have hoped, because they have not been active enough. They will have to ask their parents for permission to go out for a walk or to the park before they will be allowed to watch more TV.

Swan calls her invention "Square-eyes". She gets the name from an old saying that watching TV causes you to develop square eyes.

A. Read the clues and complete the crossword puzzle with words from the passage.

Across

A. device for measuring steps taken

B. sends

C. something never made before

D. about the care of infant and children

E. inner sole of a shoe

Down

1. tells what will happen

2. tool, instrument

3. the first form of something

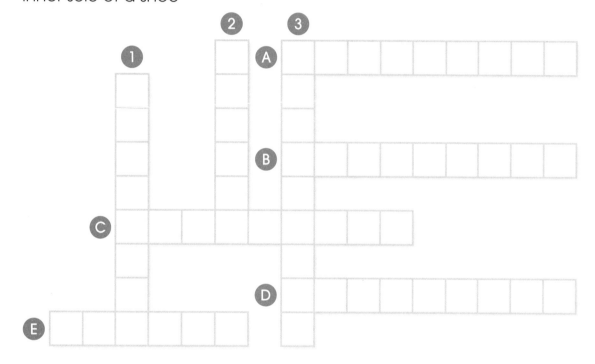

B. Write your opinion.

Should parents be able to monitor how much you walk and send you messages no matter where you are? Will this develop trust between you and your parents? Will you develop responsibility if you are always being monitored? Write a short paragraph of your views on this.

_____

_____

_____

_____

Verbs

Basically, the **verb** is for expressing action or a state of being. However, the functions of the verb go beyond that. It tells us the tense, voice, and mood of the sentence too.

> The tense of a sentence tells us when an action occurred or will occur.
> Examples: Dan <u>jumped</u> into the ditch and hurt his leg.
>   He <u>will not do</u> that again.

A. Complete the following sentences with suitable verb tenses.

1. We (go) _____ there early next week to have a look.

2. Last Saturday's concert (be) _____ not as good as I

    (expect) _____ .

3. I (not see) _____ Marcus since he moved away. It

    (be) _____ more than three years already.

4. When I (dash) _____ out, the car (speed) _____

    away already. The gang was nowhere to be found.

> The voice of a sentence shows the relationship between the verb and the subject.
> The active voice shows that the subject is doing the action whereas the passive
> voice shows that the subject is receiving the action.
> Examples: The puppy bit me.   (active voice)
>   I was bitten by the puppy.   (passive voice)

B. Change the voice in the following sentences.

1. The children picked the ripe apples.

    _____

2. The police officer warned the careless driver.

    _____

3. The books were borrowed by Sue for the project.

   _____

4. The ball was caught by the second baseman.

   _____

5. We will decorate the classroom for the party.

   _____

   _____

6. Della left the puppy in the backyard.

   _____

   _____

The mood of a sentence tells us in what manner the verb is communicating the action.

The indicative mood is used to make a basic statement or ask a question.
Example: We'll have pizza lunch at school tomorrow.

The imperative mood is used to make a command or request.
Example: Please pass the salt to me.

The subjunctive mood is used to set up a hypothetical case or express a wish.
Example: I wish I could fly.

C. Indicate the mood in each of the following sentences. Write "IN" for indicative mood, "IM" for imperative mood, and "SUB" for subjunctive mood.

1. Can you tell your sister not to disturb us when we are working?   _____

2. It is a group project that accounts for 30% of the final score.   _____

3. Go to the library to borrow some books for the project.   _____

4. We have to hand in our project before noon tomorrow.   _____

5. Matt hasn't finished compiling the data yet.   _____

6. How I wish we had more time for the project.   _____

The Golden Arches

Almost everybody has been to a McDonald's restaurant. But do you know how this famous chain started?

The current owner Ray Kroc used to sell malted milk mixing machines in the United States. One day, Ray received an order from San Bernardino for enough machines to make 40 malted milks at once. Ray was sure someone had made a mistake because no one could possibly need that many machines. Ray decided to go and check this order out, so he headed down to San Bernardino, and was absolutely amazed!

McDonald's was just a single little restaurant in the middle of a parking lot, but people were everywhere. People zipped in and out of the place getting their food in no time at all. The McDonald brothers had done something no one had ever considered before: they had made a restaurant where the food was ready even before you ordered it. Before the McDonald's fast food restaurant, it took time when people ate out. Even the cheapest restaurants did not start making your meal until after you had ordered it. The McDonald brothers had thought up something great.

Ray asked the brothers why they did not try to expand their restaurant all over the country. They told Ray that they did not want to deal with the hassle of too many restaurants, and that they already had more money than anyone would ever need.

Ray decided he wanted to be a part of the business, so he told the brothers that he would pay them a percentage of his earnings if they sold him franchise rights to the McDonald's system. This meant that Ray would be able to open different locations of McDonald's and sell its products. In April of 1955, Ray opened his first McDonald's restaurant in Chicago, and then a second in Fresno, Florida that same year. Including the McDonald brothers' restaurants in Pasadena, Los Angeles and San Bernardino, McDonald's was becoming quite the chain. It was not long before the McDonald's golden arches could be seen all over the country. In 1960, the McDonald brothers decided that they had had enough of the fast food industry, and sold the entire chain to Ray Kroc for over 2.5 million dollars.

A. Answer the following questions.

1. What prompted Ray Kroc to go to San Bernardino?

   _____

   _____

2. What made the first McDonald's restaurant so unique?

   _____

3. What was Ray Kroc able to do after securing the franchise rights to the McDonald's system?

   _____

   _____

4. Describe one thing you like or dislike about McDonald's.

   _____

   _____

B. Read the clues and unscramble the words.

1. **genarins**   profits _____

2. **selsha**   trouble _____

3. **pizped**   moved quickly _____

4. **emazda**   astonished, surprised _____

5. **daxpen**   increase the quantity _____

6. **nicha**   group of related businesses _____

7. **hisfrance**   running businesses using others' brands _____

Date : _____

Day 8

The Subjunctive Mood

We use the **subjunctive mood** to indicate a wish, a hypothetical case, a suggestion, or a demand.

Examples: If I <u>were</u> the coach, I would not let him close the game.
(Unfortunately, I am not the coach so there was no way I could stop him being the closer.)
If he <u>were</u> with us, it would be a lot more fun.
(But he wasn't with us.)
The teacher suggested that he <u>think</u> about it before getting back to her.
Her mother demanded that she <u>stay</u> home.

Note the use of "were" in indicating wishes and hypothetical cases, and the base verb in making suggestions or demands.

A. Change the verbs where necessary to reflect the subjunctive mood.

1.   If I am a billionaire, I will give you a million dollars.

_____

_____

2.   Her parents demanded that she paid for the repair.

_____

3.   We looked at him as though he is a monster.

_____

4.   How I wish Jane is here with us.

_____

5.   If I am you, I will accept the offer right away.

_____

6.   The committee proposed that Mr. Sharma took up the position of CEO.

_____

7.   If Sam is the organizer, the show would be much better.

_____

8.   If she was to leave a month earlier, she would reach her destination on time.

_____

_____

9.   The principal suggests that Matt reads more but I wonder if Matt would heed the principal's advice.

_____

_____

B.   Read the following groups of sentences. Write a sentence in the subjunctive mood to show the main idea of each group.

Example: *We all wanted Ted to play in the game. Unfortunately, Ted was sick and could not play. With Ted, we would have a better chance of winning.*

If Ted were to play in the game, we would have a better chance of winning.

1.   Valerie was busy with her project. It was past midnight but there was still a lot to do. Valerie's mother told her to leave it until the next day.

_____

_____

2.   Mr. Sherwood wants to stay fit. The doctor tells him to get up earlier and exercise for half an hour before going to work.

_____

3.   Jeremy was rude to Patricia. The teacher knew about it. She wanted Jeremy to apologize to Patricia.

_____

4.   At the party, Janet socialized with everyone that came her way. She appeared more like the hostess than a guest.

_____

The Power of One

Terry Fox had a dream: to raise a million dollars for cancer research. He grew up in Port Moody, British Columbia and had always been a great athlete. When he was only 18, he learned that he had cancer in his leg and that his leg would have to be removed. The day before the operation, Terry's basketball coach gave him a magazine. In the magazine was an article about an athlete who had his leg amputated but ran a marathon anyway. Terry was inspired. He decided that he was going to run across Canada in order to raise money for cancer research. After Terry got his first artificial leg, he began running every day to train for his run across the country.

On April 12, 1980, Terry started his "Marathon of Hope" across Canada. He started in St. John's, Newfoundland, the country's easternmost city on the shore of the Atlantic. Terry ran about 43 kilometres a day – in snow, fog, strong winds, and heat. By the time he made it to Charlottetown, he was exhausted, but he was nevertheless uplifted by all the people who were cheering for him and donating money to help fight cancer.

By September 1, Terry had to stop running because his cancer had spread to his lungs. He had to be flown back to British Columbia to undergo chemotherapy again. For 143 days and 5373 km, the determined 18-year-old had run through six provinces and was now two-thirds of the way home.

However, it seemed that Terry might not be able to realize his goal; he had to stop running. Yet people continued to donate to his cause. By February 1, 1981, the fight against cancer had already raised over 24 million dollars. Even today, people continue to donate money to Terry Fox runs.

There is a statue that marks where Terry Fox had to cut short his run. It is located just outside Thunder Bay, Ontario.

A. Read the clues and complete the crossword puzzle with words from the passage.

Across

A. encouraged
B. long-distance footrace
C. man-made
D. goal

Down

1. one who is good at sports
2. drained, very tired
3. careful study
4. cut off

B. Answer the following questions.

1. Why do you think Terry Fox named his cross-Canada run "Marathon of Hope"?

   _____

2. Where did Terry Fox reach before having to give up his run and fly back to British Columbia for treatment?

   _____

3. Why do you think Terry Fox chose to run across Canada as a way to raise money for cancer research?

   _____

4. Do you think Terry Fox had actually realized his goal? Why or why not?

   _____

   _____

   _____

Did You Know?

A very good book about Terry Fox for young readers is *Run*, which is a blend of fact and fiction by the award-winning author Eric Walters.

Date : _____

You Deserve A Break!

A. Fill in the blanks to complete the words in the teapot.

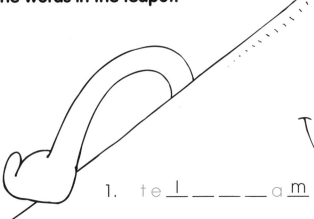

1. t e <u>l</u> __ __ __ a <u>m</u>

2. t <u>h</u> e __ __ __ __ __ a <u>t</u>

3. __ t e a <u>l</u>

4. t __ e a __ __ r __

5. t __ __ e a <u>d</u>

6. t __ e __ a <u>p</u> __

7. __ t e a <u>k</u>

8. t e a __ __ __ <u>t</u>

9. __ t e __ a __ __

10. __ t e a __ <u>y</u>

11. t __ e a <u>t</u> __ __

12. t e a __

13. t <u>o</u> __ e __ a <u>t</u> __

14. t e __ __ a <u>g</u> __

15. t __ e a __

16. __ t e a <u>m</u>

B. Colour the words that rhyme with "tea".

tree   feed

cheek   knee   bee

seal   free

me   jeep   leaf

pea   agree

key   flea   dream

sea   wheel

bean   we

three

Day **11**

Verbals

Verbals are formed from verbs but function as nouns, adjectives, or adverbs. There are three types of verbals: gerunds, participles, and infinitives.

Gerunds end in "ing" and function as nouns.

Example: <u>Fishing</u> is my father's favourite pastime in summer.

Participles are verbals that are used as adjectives.

Examples: The pirates found the <u>hidden</u> treasure. (past participle)
Shirley put on her <u>dancing</u> shoes and was all ready for the performance. (present participle)

Infinitives can be nouns, adjectives, or adverbs. They are the "to" form of verbs.

Example: <u>To win</u> the game was the only thing that mattered to them.

A. **Underline the verbals in the following sentences and state whether they are gerunds (G), participles (P), or infinitives (I).**

1. Keith wants to become a successful scientist. _____

2. We always enjoy swimming in the pool. _____

3. The cooling fan doesn't seem to work. _____

4. Judy just made herself a laughing stock. _____

5. The snow made it difficult for us to see. _____

6. To settle the debt is what concerns him most. _____

7. My mom and dad enjoy jogging in the morning. _____

8. The children greeted the crossing guard warmly. _____

9. They had their climbing ropes ready for the expedition. _____

10. Some say that cooking is an art. _____

11. They were about to leave when they heard someone knocking at the door. _____

12. Grandpa doesn't like driving at night. _____

B. Use each of the following verbs as a gerund, a participle, and an infinitive.

ski

G: _____

P: _____

I: _____

skip

G: _____

P: _____

I: _____

float

G: _____

P: _____

I: _____

shop

G: _____

P: _____

I: _____

run

G: _____

P: _____

I: _____

Levi Strauss and the Old Blue Jeans

Low rise. Patch pocket. Boot cut. Bell bottoms. Distressed. Comfort fit. All of these words bring to mind that staple of the fashion wardrobe – jeans. Songs have been written about them. Boys and girls wear them. Almost everyone owns at least one pair. Jeans have gone from merely being tough pants you wear when working to being a fashion statement.

The back pocket is the place to make the fashion statement in 2005. Little did Levi Strauss know that he was starting a fashion craze that would be alive and well even 150 years later!

It was Levi Strauss who made the very first blue jeans. During the Gold Rush in 1950, the 20-year-old Bavarian immigrant left New York for San Francisco. He thought he would make his living selling tents and wagon covers to the miners, and so brought with him bales of strong blue cloth. But as often happens to many people, he got sidetracked and responded to a challenge instead. A miner had been complaining about his trousers. Levi thought about the problem and agreed that the pants the miners were wearing did wear out too easily. He decided to respond to the need for stronger pants and created the first pair of blue jeans.

At first, Levi Strauss had canvas made into pants. Miners liked his pants, but complained that they tended to chafe. So, he substituted a twilled cotton cloth from France called "serge de Nimes", which later became known as denim.

Nowadays Levi's is not the only company making jeans, and the jeans are not all blue. The more expensive they are, the less likely they will ever be used as rugged pants for work!

A. Circle the correct answers.

1. Levi Strauss's first pants were made of _____ .

   A. denim
   B. canvas
   C. cotton
   D. serge de Nimes

2. The word "bales" means _____ .

   A. packages
   B. blankets
   C. bundles
   D. wagons

3. Levi Strauss originally planned to _____ .

   A. make blue jeans
   B. work as a miner
   C. make tents
   D. make canvas

4. The miner complained at first because he wanted pants that _____ .

   A. would look better
   B. would feel better
   C. would last longer
   D. were cheaper

B. Design a label for the back pocket of a pair of jeans and write a few sentences to sell your design to a clothing store.

_____

_____

_____

_____

_____

_____

_____

_____

_____

Day 13

Verbal Phrases

A **verbal phrase** contains a gerund, a participle, or an infinitive. It functions as a noun, an adjective, or an adverb.

Examples: The winning pitcher waved at the cheering crowd.
Fishing in the bitter cold is a test of will.
He doesn't want to leave her behind.

A.   Underline the verbal phrase(s) in each of the following sentences.

1. Dad took us on a skiing trip.

2. Skiing downhill was much more difficult than I had thought.

3. It was difficult to keep my balance on the slippery slope.

4. The little children enjoyed tobogganing more than skiing.

5. Exhausted after the practice, we suggested taking a rest.

6. Without the skiing pants, we would have been frozen to death.

7. Drinking a cup of hot chocolate was the best reward after the first skiing lesson.

8. My sister looked helpless sitting on the snow.

9. She discovered something buried deep in the snow.

10. It was a torn mitten!

B. **State whether each infinitive below is used as a noun (N), an adjective (ADJ), or an adverb (ADV).**

1. <u>To complete</u> the work in one day is near impossible.   _____

2. She wanted <u>to learn</u> knitting.   _____

3. The children went home <u>to eat</u> their supper.   _____

4. Her mother made her a hat <u>to wear</u> at the party.   _____

5. The team weren't ready <u>to quit</u>.   _____

C. **Write sentences using the following gerund, participle, or infinitive phrases.**

1. skating on the frozen pond

    _____

2. stuck in the traffic jam

    _____

3. writing a journal entry

    _____

4. to be a good basketball player

    _____

5. enjoying a lazy afternoon

    _____

6. to write an e-mail

    _____

7. tired of waiting

    _____

    _____

8. camping in the provincial park

    _____

    _____

    _____

The McIntosh Apple

The McIntosh apple is a bright red, crisp, and sweet tasting apple that is a common and popular fruit in every grocery store in Canada today. Every McIntosh apple tree today stems from a single tree discovered on a farm near Prescott, Ontario owned by a man named John McIntosh in 1811.

While clearing the land for his farm, McIntosh discovered about 20 young apple trees. Apples were one of the few fruits available to pioneers in Canada and the United States, so he transplanted the trees to a garden near his home. One of these trees produced apples that were bright red, crisp, and sweet.

These apples were enjoyed by many of John's friends and neighbours. But to their dismay, they learned that when planting the seeds from the core and even when bees pollinated the apple tree, the tree which grew did not produce the same red apples. Later, a farmhand showed John's son, Allen, how to cut small tree branches called scions and tie, or graft, them to another tree to grow the McIntosh.

Allen, the ninth son of John's 13 children, became a weekend Methodist preacher. He took with him a number of McIntosh apples when he went out preaching to distant communities. He also began grafting parts of the tree so that it could be grown in other places by other farmers.

In 1845, Allen took over his father's farm, and his younger brother Sandy became a teacher of grafting techniques and salesperson for the farms in Eastern Ontario. By Confederation in 1867, some farmers no longer grew multiple crops and focused solely on growing apple trees. This exclusive growing of apples on farms caused them to become known as apple orchards.

Harvey Austin, Sandy's son, expanded the small apple orchard by marketing thousands of trees all over Ontario and even the northern United States. By 1910, McIntosh apples were being sold in British Columbia. The McIntosh is even used to breed apples such as Cortland, Joyce, and Melba.

If you ever need to think of a Canadian dish, think McIntosh apple pie!

A. Write "T" for the true statements and "F" for the false ones.

1. Only the original apple tree could produce red, crisp, and sweet apples. _____

2. Cortland, Joyce, and Melba all came from McIntosh. _____

3. Grafting parts of the original apple tree enabled it to be grown in other places. _____

4. John McIntosh was one of the pioneers settling in Canada. _____

5. The McIntosh apple originated in the province of British Columbia. _____

6. During pioneer days, farmers grew multiple crops. _____

B. Read the clues and complete the crossword puzzle with words from the passage.

Across

A. moved plants and grew them somewhere else

B. concentrated

C. disappointment

D. small tree branches

Down

1. skills

2. worker on a farm

3. early settlers

Day 15

Some Vexing Agreements

When putting together a sentence, we need to make sure that the words correspond in both person and number, or "agree" with one another.

Examples: The functions of this nifty MP3 player is listed on the manual. (✗)
The function<u>s</u> of this nifty MP3 player <u>are</u> listed on the manual. (✔)
Marilyn, Sue, and I am going to the trip together. (✗)
Marilyn, Sue, and I <u>are</u> going to the trip together. (✔)
Neither the passengers nor the driver were aware of it. (✗)
Neither the passengers nor the driver <u>was</u> aware of it. (✔)

A. Circle the correct choice in each of the following sentences.

1. Everyone (like / likes) the model we built.

2. (One / Some) of the ingredients is not really that suitable.

3. Mr. Simmons, together with all his students, (is / are) going to sing at the concert.

4. Neither the waiters nor the chef (know / knows) what's going on.

5. (Each / All) of them are happy to hear about their sister's success.

6. Anybody who (spell / spells) the words correctly will be given a prize.

7. Both you and I (are / am) held responsible for the wrongdoing.

8. Either the workmen or the supervisor (was / were) at fault.

9. I don't think anyone in class (practise / practises) it every day.

10. The children, except Ron, (has / have) agreed to work on it.

11. There (is / are) just a few cookies left.

12. (One / Several) of the windows has been broken.

B. **Read the following sentences. Rewrite those containing faulty agreements.**

1. Either you or I are eligible for the scholarship.

   _____

2. The cell phone with all the bells and whistles comes with a hefty price.

   _____

3. The coach, as well as the players, were very disappointed with the decision.

   _____

4. Each of the children were given a basket of strawberries.

   _____

5. No one seems to pay any attention to the performance.

   _____

6. Neither the class nor the teacher have heard of the news.

   _____

7. None of the committee members were prepared to vote.

   _____

8. Have any one of you met our new principal before?

   _____

9. Neither of them was brave enough to take up the challenge.

   _____

10. None of the houses have been damaged.

    _____

11. Someone holding three parcels at the door want to talk to you.

    _____

    _____

12. Everyone attending the wedding ceremony were happy for them.

    _____

The CN Tower – the World's Tallest Structure

One of Ontario's prime tourist attractions is the CN Tower. It is the tallest freestanding structure in the world, and will probably remain so because satellite broadcasting has replaced the need to build tall broadcast towers. At the time, it cost $63 000 000 to build this telecommunications hub. To build it in today's market with the current costs of materials and labour, the tower would probably cost $300 000 000!

It took 1500 workers to complete the structure. They worked 24 hours a day, five days a week, for 40 months. Obviously the workers worked in shifts! Made of reinforced concrete at 185 storeys high, the tower reaches 533 metres into the clouds. That makes for one impressive building!

The world's largest helicopter, the Sikorski from Russia, put the final antenna mast in place. On the day of completion, an ironworker named Paul Mitchell was there at the top of the structure to guide the pole into place and signal the helicopter to release the guide wires. He climbed out of the structure, held on to a lightning rod, and waved to the people below! Imagine the nerves of steel you need to be an ironworker working on skyscrapers! You needed a zoom lens on your camera to see him.

The CN Tower is called the "Jewel of Toronto". It was opened to the public on June 26, 1976, and has two million visitors a year. Tourists travel up the tower in glass elevators to one or all of the four lookout levels. Located at a height of 342 m is the glass floor and outdoor Observation Deck. There are 60 millimetres of glass between you and the ground. The glass is actually stronger than the concrete floor. Some people lie on the floor to get the feeling that there is nothing between them and the ground!

360 is the name of the restaurant located at 351 m. It offers guests a complete 360-degree view of the city. The floor in the restaurant rotates once every 72 minutes allowing a complete and unobstructed view of Toronto while you are dining. By the time your meal is complete, you will have completed your revolution of the city and the surrounding area. What a way to tour the region!

A. **List five facts and five opinions about the CN Tower from the passage.**

1. _____

2. _____

3. _____

4. _____

5. _____

1. _____

2. _____

3. _____

4. _____

5. _____

B. **Answer the following questions.**

1. Why is it not likely that some other country will build a taller tower than the CN Tower?

_____

2. Do you think the 360 restaurant is well named? Think of what you have learned in math class.

_____

3. The CN Tower is called the "Jewel of Toronto". What do you think is the "Jewel of Canada"? Explain your answer.

_____

_____

_____

_____

Did You Know?

The CN Tower's metal staircases – 1776 steps, or 147 storeys – are only open to the public twice a year, for charity stairclimb events: organized by the World Wildlife Fund in spring, and by the United Way in fall.

Relative Pronouns and Interrogative Pronouns

We use a **relative pronoun** to connect a dependent clause to the main clause.

Examples: 1.   The player is my cousin. <u>He</u> hit two homeruns.
The player <u>who</u> hit two homeruns is my cousin.

2.   This is my cousin. I haven't seen <u>her</u> for years.
This is my cousin <u>whom</u> I haven't seen for years.

3.   The dress was reduced to half price. She bought <u>the dress</u>.
The dress <u>that</u> she bought was reduced to half price.

4.   The diagram is now on display. We drew the <u>diagram</u>.
The diagram <u>which</u> we drew is now on display.

A.   Complete the following sentences with suitable relative pronouns.

1.   The kitten _____ we fed belongs to Joanne.

2.   I met the man _____ I had mentioned to you last week.

3.   She borrowed the book _____ I wanted.

4.   He was the one _____ did it all by himself.

5.   They joined the tour _____ lasted a week.

6.   We took the route _____ led to a deserted farmhouse.

B.   Join the following pairs of sentences with relative pronouns.

1.   The teacher likes the picture. Jamie drew the picture.

_____

2.   The teacher is leaving us. Everyone admires the teacher.

_____

_____

3. We watched a film. The film was about the discovery of America.

_____

_____

_____

4. The young man is his brother. The young man works part-time as a lifeguard.

_____

_____

5. The dish won the grand award. Her mother cooked the dish.

_____

_____

6. The tree now stands taller than I. We planted the tree last summer.

_____

_____

C. **Choose the correct interrogative pronoun to complete each of the following questions.**

1. (Who, Whom) _____ do you think is responsible for the accident?

2. (Which, Who) _____ pumpkin is the heaviest on record?

> We use interrogative pronouns **to ask questions.**

3. For (whom, who) _____ are you doing this?

4. At (which, whose) _____ stop should we get off?

5. (Whose, Who) _____ dog won the trophy?

6. (Who, Which) _____ cleaned up all the mess for us?

7. (Which, Whom) _____ school will organize this year's inter-school marathon?

8. Do you know to (who, whom) _____ I should hand this letter?

The Poppy – a Symbol for Remembrance Day

"In Flanders Fields" is a poem that all Canadian school children learn to recite on November 11, Remembrance Day, every year. It was written by a Canadian doctor named John McCrae. He was a member of the Canadian Army Medical Corps during the First World War. He died of pneumonia while serving in France in 1918, the year the war ended. This famous Canadian was born in Guelph and his birthplace is now a museum and a national historic site.

In the poem, McCrae mentions the red poppies that grow wild in the fields of France and Belgium. In the line from the poem which states: "...between the crosses, row on row that mark our place", the author contrasts the beauty of the red poppies growing naturally in the fields to the starkness of the rows of graves of fallen soldiers. Because of this poem, the Canadian Veterans Associations chose the poppy as a symbol of remembrance for the soldiers who died in wars for Canada. People wear poppies on November 11 as a sign of recognition and remembrance for the sacrifice of those who died fighting for freedom.

The John McCrae Museum in Guelph is surrounded by many varieties of the poppy species that bloom in the gardens and in the park. The museum staff planted them to remind people of the poppies in the fields in France. The poppies in France and Belgium have red petals with a centre of black stamens. They are hard to miss when you travel the countryside. They fill the fields like dandelions do here in Canada.

The Veterans Associations sell the poppy symbols on November 11. They use the money raised to help amputees. Amputees are people who have lost a limb and need a prothesis, a mechanical device to replace the limb. On Remembrance Day, proudly wear a red poppy on your chest to remember the soldiers who died in wars.

A. Answer the following questions.

1. "This famous Canadian was born in Guelph and his birthplace is now a museum and a national historic site." What does the word "site" mean?

_____

_____

2. "They fill the fields like dandelions do here in Canada." Do you think poppies are hard to grow? Explain.

_____

_____

3. "The Veterans Associations sell the poppy symbols on November 11." How would you define the word "symbol"?

_____

_____

4. Explain what "sacrifice" means in "the sacrifice of the soldiers who died fighting for freedom."

_____

_____

B. Write a paragraph on why people wear poppies on Remembrance Day. Support your answer with sentences from the passage.

_____

_____

_____

_____

_____

_____

_____

Did You Know?

It was French YMCA Secretary Madame Guerin who conceived the idea of selling poppies to help needy soldiers.

Day
19

Commas

We use a **comma** to:

- separate words or phrases in a series.

  Example: I enjoy playing hockey, baseball, and basketball.

- separate adjectives before a noun.

  Example: She wore a long, satin dress to the party.

- separate a dependent clause from an independent clause when the dependent clause appears first in the sentence.

  Example: When they heard the news, they broke into tears.

- set off transitional words.

  Example: However, I ignored him and continued with my work.

- set off a direct quotation.

  Example: Jeremy said to him, "You'd better finish it on time."

- set off words in apposition.

  Example: Our teacher, Mr. Weir, will teach at another school next term.

A. Add commas where needed in the following sentences.

1. The farmer gave us some carrots a few apples and a lot of potatoes.

2. Of course they won't let him join the game again.

3. Indeed it was the best we could do for her.

4. The incident happened on June 19 2004.

5. Once we start we should continue and not give up.

6. Although I didn't see it happen I could feel the horror.

7. The little boy replied "I just asked for some candies."

8. Did you see the sleek blue sports car on the driveway?

9. Mrs. Thomson our next door neighbour told us not to worry.

10. The storm left the village with flooded basements fallen trees and mudslides.

Using Commas to Set off Non-defining Clauses

We use commas to set off a non-defining clause in a sentence. A non-defining clause is one that adds information but is not a necessary part of the sentence.

Example: The coach, <u>who is a native of Windsor</u>, doesn't think that they stand a chance in the play-off.

We do not use commas to set off a defining clause because a defining clause is essential to defining the noun described.

Example: I need the book <u>that explains weather and climate</u> to complete the project.

B. Decide which of the following sentences contain non-defining clauses. Add commas where needed.

1. Our dog which everyone loves likes eating snacks.

2. The show that he wanted to watch was not telecast.

3. The teachers who play in the game will practise tomorrow at the gym.

4. On my way to school, I ran into Jim's mother who told me that Jim was not feeling well.

5. Don't you want to be someone that everybody admires?

6. She let me see her camera which was as thin as a credit card.

7. I know a place where we can play hide-and-seek.

8. Never trust a stranger who offers you a ride home.

9. He is a player whom everyone looks up to.

10. The tools that we need for the repair work are stored in the shed over there.

11. Pam's younger sister who looks very much like her will come to the party too.

12. Mrs. Steele whose son is about my age bakes great cookies.

Date : _____

Day 20

You Deserve A Break!

Help the scientists transform each word block by writing another word with the same letters.

1. rate
2. there
3. team
4. heart
5. stoat
6. diary
7. react
8. rose
9. early
10. cents
11. name
12. use
13. from
14. wand
15. coal
16. loaf
17. acre
18. hear
19. feel
20. ring

1. _____
2. _____
3. _____
4. _____
5. _____
6. _____
7. _____
8. _____
9. _____
10. _____
11. _____
12. _____
13. _____
14. _____
15. _____
16. _____
17. _____
18. _____
19. _____
20. _____

A Canadian Artist and a War Memorial

The monument at the Canadian National Vimy Memorial Park in France is almost 70 years old. Inscribed on the ramparts of the monument are the names of 11 285 Canadian soldiers who were posted "missing, presumed dead" in France. Though the Memorial is on French soil, it has been designated a national historic site of Canada, and is the work of the Toronto artist and architect Walter S. Allward.

Allward was never formally trained as an artist. When he was young, he attended Saturday classes at the Ontario College of Art. He once told his friends that the design of the Vimy Memorial came to him in a dream.

The monument is a massive structure of two tall monoliths with male and female figures at the base. Some suggest the towers represent gateways to the heavens. The figure representing Canada is that of a young woman with a bowed head to symbolize mourning. The figure holds a laurel branch in a downward position at the end of her arm. Though the laurel has been the symbol of victory since Greek and Roman times, the way she holds it at her side shows a sense of loss. It took too many lives to achieve victory. This was a very high price for a young nation to pay.

Both the monument and the battle are noteworthy for Canadians. The Vimy Memorial stands on Hill 145 in France, overlooking the Canadian battlefield of 1917 during the First World War. This is the site of one of the fiercest battles fought. It was a turning point of the war and essential to stopping Germany's advance. The grounds are still honeycombed with wartime tunnels where the soldiers used to sleep.

When Allward arrived at the site in 1922, trees had grown on the battlefield and his workers had to build a road. Allward spent years looking for the right stone to carve the figures. In the end, he selected a limestone from Yugoslavia. The figure representing Canada is carved from a single block. Work began on the monument in 1925 and, 11 years later on July 26, 1936, the Memorial was unveiled by King Edward VIII.

Ironically, Allward's monument took so long to build that by the time it was completed, the Second World War was about to break out. The First World War was referred to as "the war to end all wars", but in fact it was not. The monument remains a reminder that we must always work towards preserving world peace.

A. Answer the following questions.

1. Why is the young woman's head bowed?

   _____

   _____

2. What do laurel leaves traditionally symbolize?

   _____

3. Canadian troops won the battle of Vimy. Why does the woman in the monument hold the laurel leaves down instead of high in the air?

   _____

   _____

Visualization

One way to improve our reading skills is to visualize what we read. Creating a mental picture helps us to focus, remember, and apply our learning in new situations. Visualizing helps us to better understand the emotions conveyed.

B. Pretend that you were a WWI veteran revisiting the battlefield at Vimy. Use five or six sentences to express the emotions you might feel.

Think about your comrades, the noise of battle, the sound of the horses injured and the sound of shells exploding.

_____

_____

_____

_____

_____

_____

_____

More on Commas

It is wrong to separate two independent clauses with a comma. There are three ways to correct it:

1.   Change one independent clause to a dependent clause.
2.   Use a conjunction to join the two independent clauses.
3.   Create two sentences.

Example: I had waited there for three hours, she did not turn up.

      1.   Although I had waited there for three hours, she did not turn up.

      2.   I had waited there for three hours but she did not turn up.

      3.   I had waited there for three hours. She did not turn up.

A.   Rewrite the following sentences to correct the wrong use of commas.

1.   It was a truly memorable event, everyone had a good time.

    _____

    _____

2.   The game went down to the bottom of the ninth inning, we didn't lose hope.

    _____

    _____

3.   I answered the door, an old man handed me a parcel.

    _____

4.   When they went in, they saw a man in his late 30s, he was dressing the wound in his leg.

    _____

    _____

5.   The road was slippery, the truck slid into a ditch, luckily, the driver was not hurt.

    _____

    _____

6. I put the book on the top shelf, someone must have taken it away.

_____

7. After knowing that we will soon face the toughest team, the coach wants us to practise more, only then can we stand a chance of winning.

_____

_____

8. If they began earlier, they might be able to finish it, there is simply not enough time now.

_____

_____

B. **Circle the commas that are wrongly used in the following paragraph about Wayne Gretzky. Rewrite the sentences that need to be reorganized using the three ways shown at the beginning.**

In his first season of organized hockey, Gretzky managed to score just one goal, however, in his second season, he scored 27, and 104 in his third season. By the time Wayne was ten, he scored an astounding 378 goals in a single season.

Wayne's idol was Gordie Howe, Howe was with the Detroit Red Wings, he held numerous scoring titles.
Little did Wayne know that he would go on to break all of his idol's records, he would set new ones that seem insurmountable even today.

_____

_____

_____

_____

_____

_____

_____

_____

What's Your Point of View?

Grace always feels funny on Remembrance Day. She wants to be proud of being Canadian, but her Japanese heritage makes her feel unsure. Her great-great grandfather emigrated to Canada in 1871 and was one of the 15 000 Chinese and Japanese who worked on building the Canadian Pacific Railway. The work was gruelling and dangerous, and many died.

Grace is proud of her great-great grandfather's contribution to building the Canadian nation. But from 1939 to1945, the Japanese people who lived in British Columbia were put into camps. They were accused of being spies and enemy agents. This was humiliating for Grace's ancestors, many of whom were born in Canada.

Her mother said, "When the Japanese bombed Pearl Harbour in Hawaii, everyone was shocked! The Americans didn't think they would be attacked because they were far away from where the war was being fought. The attack caused people to be even more scared of the war."

"Even though they had never been to Japan, my great-grandparents were accused of being spies and had to leave their home and their flower business," her mother continued. "This happened to all the Japanese in British Columbia. The government sold off their businesses and homes. After the war they were left with nothing. They didn't get an apology from the government until 1989!"

"Didn't other people help them?" Grace sounded shocked.

"A war was going on," her mother said gravely. "Many thought that some people's liberty had to be sacrificed. It wasn't fair. They let worry and fear cause them to be racist."

"What was it like for the Japanese back then?" Grace asked curiously.

"They were housed in wooden barracks and many had to work on sugar beet farms," her mother answered." They lost their freedom. The worst part was that even after the war, they didn't get their land and businesses back. Imagine having to start all over again from scratch."

A. Select explicit details.

One way to decide what is most important in what we read is to do the following activity:

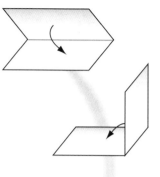

Take a piece of loose-leaf paper. Fold it in half; then fold the half again. Fold it one more time in half. When you open the paper, it is divided into eight folds or divisions.

- Write one detail about Grace's story in each fold.
- Now tear the paper into eight sections.
- Discard the two least important details.
- Read over all the remaining sections.
- Discard two more that you consider to be less important.
- You are now left with four important main points about the article.
- Record them in the spaces below.

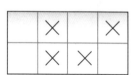

1. _____

2. _____

3. _____

4. _____

B. Write your point of view.

When reading this story, you formed an opinion on what Grace's ancestors experienced. Use the explicit details you selected to help you create arguments that support or oppose what Grace thinks.

_____

_____

_____

_____

_____

Colons and Semicolons

Colons

We use a **colon**:

- to introduce a list of items or a quotation.
- to set off a concluding statement.
- between a title and a subtitle.
- between two clauses when the second one explains the first.

A.   Add colons where needed in the following sentences.

1. The chairman neglected one crucial fact the report was not ready.

2. We all have the same goal win the tournament this time.

3. The old saying goes "Blood is thicker than water."

4. They were told to pack these for the trip a flashlight, a compass, and a radio.

5. The company had the following openings secretary, receptionist, administrative assistant.

6. The article "Travel in Asia China and India" is an interesting read.

7. We expect only one thing from him complete the project by next Monday.

8. Do remember this never ever give up.

9. He came up with a brilliant idea combine the two into one.

10. The instructor told us to get ready these items a glove, a bat, a helmet, and a few baseballs.

B.   Write two sentences using the colon.

1. _____

2. _____

Semicolons

We use a **semicolon**:
– in place of a conjunction to join two closely related clauses or sentences.
– between a series of items when the items are long or contain commas within.

C. Add semicolons where needed in the following sentences.

1. To prepare himself for the race, he performed the following exercises every day: weightlifting, which built his upper body strength running, which built up his endurance biking, which strengthened his leg muscles.

2. They met with John it was a brief meeting.

3. He was introduced to the following people: Jason, Peter's cousin Mandy, his boss's daughter Sam, the secretary's husband.

4. It was chilly out there the temperature dropped to a mere 2°C.

5. We tried our best to finish it on time however, we couldn't make it.

6. She's such a popular athlete wherever she goes, she's surrounded by fans.

7. He found himself face to face with someone he knew it was Corey.

8. The surprise gift finally arrived it was a nifty DVD player.

9. No one wanted to leave they were all eager for the announcement.

10. We had a sumptuous dinner everyone was full.

D. Write two sentences using the semicolon.

1. _____

2. _____

Date : _____

The Black Loyalists

Jemal has a different cultural past than his friends. His ancestors have lived in Nova Scotia since 1779. He is a ninth generation Canadian! That is pretty impressive in a country where many of the kids in school have parents who were not born in Canada.

In 1775, the Americans went to war with the British in what is known as the American Revolution. They wanted to become a country instead of being a colony of Britain. The Governor of Virginia passed a proclamation promising freedom to any slave who would escape from his rebel master and fight on the side of those loyal to the British Crown.

Black Soldiers fought in the belief that they were securing freedom. The British promised grants of land and provisions to the former slaves once the rebellion was defeated. It is estimated that as many as 100 000 slaves joined the army because of that promise. By the summer of 1782, it became evident that the Americans were winning the war. The British offered to send more than 3500 Black Loyalists to Nova Scotia and New Brunswick.

The people who remained loyal to the British King at the time were called "Loyalists". The Americans called themselves "Patriots" because they were trying to break away from Britain to establish their own country. Though Black Loyalists who came to Nova Scotia were promised the same treatment as the White Loyalists, that was not in fact the case. Blacks were forced to settle in areas located outside main towns. They had great difficulties in getting their land grants, and were not accepted by many of the White Loyalists as their equals.

In spite of the difficulties, these people who had been slaves eventually started on the road to independence. In the war of 1812, there were three black battalions fighting on the Canadian side. Jemal has every right to be proud of his ancestors' contribution to building Canada.

This passage presents one side, or viewpoint, on the Loyalists. If you were an American, you would have one point of view and if you were British, you would have another.

A. If you had been a slave in 18th century America, would you have been loyal to Britain, or would you have joined the American side? Present your opinion and use details such as facts and examples to support it.

_____

_____

_____

_____

_____

B. In the "I Read" column, list three points you learned from the passage. Write your opinion opposite each point in the "I think" column. Then draw a conclusion in the "Therefore" section.

I Read...

I Think...

Therefore...

Did You Know?

The Kids Book of Black Canadian History by Rosemary Sadlier talks about how black people came to Canada from different countries. It includes stories about the slavery in New France, the Black Loyalists, and the Underground Railroad.

Date : _____

Day 26

Dashes and Hyphens

Dashes

We use a **dash** to:

– separate a series at the beginning of a sentence from its explanatory section.

Example: A compass, a radio, and a flashlight – these are the essentials we need for our hike.

– set off a description or comment that is meant to further the reader's understanding of the sentence.

Example: The science project – the most difficult of all – will account for 40% of the total score.

– set off an elaboration of an idea at the end of a sentence.

Example: They had only one thing in mind – winning the game.

A.   Rewrite the following sentences, adding dashes where needed.

1. The final showdown the do-or-die game will be telecast live.

_____

2. Everything boiled down to one word perseverance.

_____

3. The Greatest Game Ever Played the story of an underdog golfer is the best motivational film I have ever watched.

_____

_____

4. No matter what you do explaining, pleading, or begging won't make her change her mind.

_____

_____

5. Digital cameras, cell phones, and MP3 players these are gadgets we almost can't do without.

_____

_____

Hyphens

We use a **hyphen** to join compound words, divide a word into syllables, or indicate a split in a word at the end of a line.

Examples: Compound adjectives: a well-liked teacher, a larger-than-life figure
Compound numbers: fifty-five, one-fifth
Prefixes: anti-social, re-sign (to sign again, as opposed to "resign")

B. Rewrite the following sentences, adding hyphens where needed.

1. The new manager is a twenty three year old graduate.

    _____

2. This is a once in a lifetime chance that you shouldn't miss.

    _____

3. Non members are not allowed to go in the members only lounge.

    _____

4. The semi final for the above eighteen contestants will start next week.

    _____

5. He lives in a twenty five year old split level bungalow.

    _____

6. A lot of people were inspired by his from rags to riches story.

    _____

7. The report shows that two thirds of the population are under fifty five years of age.

    _____

    _____

8. The pro government rally was held a block away from the anti government protest.

    _____

    _____

The Ghost of Cherry Hill House

Cherry Hill House Restaurant in Mississauga, Ontario was built on the site of an ancient burial ground of Canada's First People. But that is not the only piece of history on the site.

The restaurant itself was converted from one of the first farmhouses in the area. Long ago, the house was the home of the first settlers to the area. It was preserved and moved to its present site to become a restaurant.

This tale takes place during the reconstruction of the house into a restaurant. Every night the construction workers who were working on the house would leave their tools in the attic on the third floor when they left the job site. Normally, carpenters and labourers look after their tools. They store them carefully at the end of the workday so they will not be damaged. Each night the carpenters would lock their tools in their metal tool chests. Some mornings they would return to find the tools scattered all over the attic on the third floor. The job site was secure. The restaurant was locked and a security guard patrolled the grounds. How did the tools end up all over the attic?

But that is not the end of the strange happenings. Other unexplained occurrences have happened there. Once the restaurant was completed and operating, the manager would report strange things if he or she stayed past midnight working in the attic office on the third floor. More than one manager have reported seeing a woman in a long, old-fashioned white dress on the third floor. This apparition is only sighted if someone works after midnight.

Would you want to work there?

A. Support your own opinion.

Do you believe in ghosts? What evidence from the passage is there to support your opinion? Using point form, write down all the information that suggests unusual things are happening under "Fact". Under "Opinion", write your own conclusions about the events.

Fact

_____

_____

_____

_____

_____

Opinion

_____

_____

_____

_____

_____

B. Based on what you have written above, use the passage and your own ideas to explain why you believe or do not believe in ghosts.

_____

_____

_____

More Punctuation Devices

Parentheses

We use **parentheses** to enclose additional information.

Example: The Mennonites (with a dwindling population) settle mostly in St. Jacobs Country, Ontario.

Parentheses may also be used to add a comment to a statement.

Example: California (see Figure 2) is a state along the Pacific Ocean.

We can also use parentheses to show letters and numbers that designate a series of items.

Example: Before leaving, remember to (a) switch off all the lights (b) close all the windows and (c) lock the door.

A. **Place parentheses where needed in the following sentences.**

1. The new museum see inset will be officially opened on August 21, 2007.

2. The honour students of which I am one are invited to the ceremony.

3. The complimentary tickets a pair from Uncle Charlie and another pair from Mr. Todd came just in time.

4. They should a get a form b fill it out c get their parents' consent and d return it to their teacher before noon tomorrow.

5. The merger yet to be confirmed is said to take effect in January 2007.

6. The graph Fig. 2b shows the population growth over the past 20 years.

7. The series 2-2 would be decided in the final game to be played this afternoon.

8. The supporting role Captain Truman was given to a little-known actor by the name of Willie Whitt.

Ellipsis Dots

We use **ellipsis dots** to shorten a quotation when the quotation is longer than what we need.

Example: It is stated clearly in Clause 3: "… with the consent of the director and three board members."

B. Add ellipsis dots with "∧" where needed in the following sentences.

1. Recent research indicates that most of the asteroids orbit around the chance that an asteroid strikes the Earth is one in a million.

2. Malls sprout up in big cities due to the largest shopping centre in the world is the West Edmonton Mall in Edmonton.

3. Malawi is an impoverished third world country in Africa. The infant mortality rate the average life expectancy is only 37 years.

4. There are many ways to conserve energy with more and more people switch to driving smaller cars which are more fuel-efficient.

5. Roberta Bondar became the first female astronaut to go into space. She received the Order of Canada In 1998, Roberta was named to the Canadian Medical Hall of Fame.

6. The cell phone has become almost an indispensable gadget the government is beginning to look into regulating the use of the cell phone.

7. A Great White ranges from five to seven metres in length and weighs swimming at a speed of 16 to 20 km per hour, the Great White usually attacks its prey from behind or beneath.

The Titanic

Do you believe in ghosts? Ghost stories are told about many places and people. Canada has its own tales of terror and mystery. Did you know the Titanic went down off the edge of Newfoundland's Grand Banks?

The Titanic was named after one of the giants from Greek myths. It was built by the White Star Shipping Company, and was supposed to be the most modern and the safest ship on the sea at that time. Launched on April 10, 1912, this luxurious ocean liner left the British port of Southampton with 2227 people aboard. It also carried the mummified body of an ancient Egyptian princess who had been a member of the Cult of the Dead during Egyptian times. She had lived and died around 1050 B.C. Did the mummified princess bring a curse on the voyage of the Titanic?

The Titanic collided with an enormous iceberg just moments after the iceberg was sighted at 11:40 p.m. on April 14, 1912. This mammoth ship, that was supposed to be so safe, sank completely and rapidly and led to the deaths of 1522 people. The passengers either drowned or froze to death in the icy waters off Newfoundland.

The ocean liner was supposed to be one of the best made ships for its time. Do you think the ancient body it was carrying had anything to do with the tragedy?

A. **Find each of the following words in the passage and underline the complete sentence. Then use the sense of the sentence to write what you think the word means.**

1. luxurious _____

2. launched _____

3. mummified _____

4. ancient _____

5. curse _____

6. enormous _____

7. mammoth _____

Drawing Conclusions

Readers draw conclusions based on the ideas and information that they read. Let's make an Agree/Disagree chart to organize the information from the passage first.

B. First, list some key points from the passage. Then indicate whether you agree or disagree with the statements. Finally, make comments of your own.

I read...	Agree ✔ Disagree ✘	Comments
The ship was supposed to be the best ship for its time.	✔	How could it have sunk so fast?

Based on your chart above, what conclusions can you make?

_____

_____

Day 30

YOU Deserve A Break!

A. Circle fifteen "space" words in the word search.

a	j	h	M	p	i	s	g	o	k	n	l	v	r	d	t	q	c
k	o	m	p	c	t	u	x	e	M	y	s	p	h	z	n	E	t
d	a	s	t	r	o	n	o	m	y	e	y	r	t	i	a	f	
f	N	p	r	m	b	l	h	w	r	w	r	N	S	l	q	r	a
t	u	a	d	x	o	v	g	v	q	n	t	c	m	v	M	t	k
g	j	c	i	h	y	p	x	l	N	e	p	t	u	n	e	h	o
v	p	e	s	u	o	E	g	v	i	z	s	b	p	r	y	g	N
b	a	s	t	e	r	o	i	d	t	g	a	l	a	x	y	v	l
N	w	h	z	c	b	o	o	e	w	S	r	t	o	m	w	p	d
h	r	i	m	p	i	x	c	y	q	l	e	z	m	o	o	n	u
n	w	p	r	w	t	N	g	k	z	o	y	c	j	r	h	i	f
p	e	z	S	E	r	n	s	b	e	v	t	y	q	u			
l	y	j	s	a	t	e	l	l	i	t	e	w	k				
a	M	o	w	n	t	m	w	h	x	n	z	r					
n	k	p	l	x	p	u	c	z	l	j	N	s					
e	u	i	r	g	M	a	r	s	c	m	p	b					
t	e	c	x	s	f	j	E	n	u	g	k						
a	E	m	a	o	d	y	p	a	q	i	e						

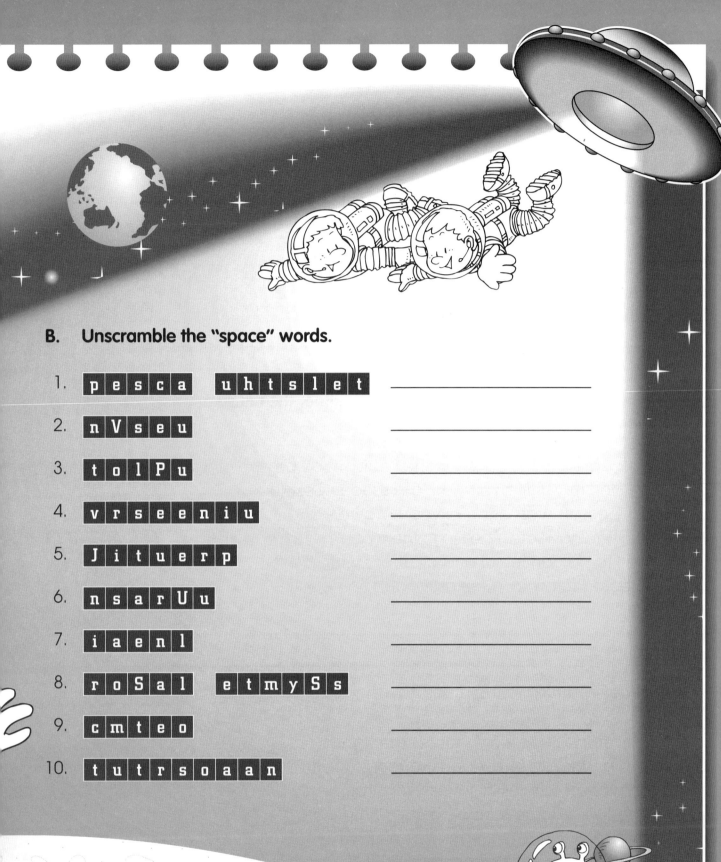

B. Unscramble the "space" words.

1. p e s c a   u h t s l e t _____

2. n V s e u _____

3. t o l P u _____

4. v r s e e n i u _____

5. J i t u e r p _____

6. n s a r U u _____

7. i a e n l _____

8. r o S a l   e t m y S s _____

9. c m t e o _____

10. t u t r s o a a n _____

Day
31

Cause and Effect

A **cause** is the reason why something happens. An **effect** is what happens. A cause results in an effect and an effect is the result of a cause.

Example: Thanks to technological advancement, we can stay connected wherever we are by way of e-mail, instant messaging, or cell phone.

Cause: Technological advancement

Effect: We can stay connected wherever we are.

Read the following paragraphs and identify either the cause or the effect.

1. The Apollo 13 mission to the moon was progressing uneventfully until an oxygen tank suddenly exploded. The spacecraft was losing oxygen, power, and its ability to navigate. The trip to the moon's surface had to be cancelled and all efforts were being directed to bringing the astronauts home safely.

    Cause: _____

    _____

    Effect: The trip to the moon's surface was cancelled.

2. Johnstone Strait is famous for the sighting of orcas. In July and August every year, the number of whales in Johnstone Strait peaks due to the large schools of salmon passing through. Since salmon is one of whales' favourite foods, they naturally make it one of their main foraging territories.

    Cause: Lots of salmon pass through Johnstone Strait in July and August every year.

    Effect: _____

    _____

3. There are 46 chromosomes in 23 pairs in each nucleus of each cell in our body. The chromosomes come in pairs because they represent the combined contribution of the father and the mother from whom we get our characteristics. That's why we look like our parents and possess some of their traits.

Cause: _____

_____

_____

Effect: We bear some of the traits of our parents.

4. Earthquakes are nature's most devastating phenomenon. They are a result of stress within the Earth which bends the Earth's crustal plates. These plates eventually split, causing "faults" that are followed by vibrations of varying degree. It is these vibrations that we call earthquakes.

In 1775, a major earthquake killed 70 000 people in Portugal and ruined the city of Lisbon. It was after the disaster that scientists started to study earthquake activities and develop instruments to monitor them. This branch of science is called seismology.

a. Cause: The stress within the Earth bends the crustal plates.

Effect: _____

_____

b. Cause: _____

_____

Effect: Scientists started to study earthquakes.

Sasquatch – Canada's Legendary Monster

Have you heard of a large hairy monster that lives in the woods and walks upright like a human? In some parts of Canada, it is called "Big Foot" because of the large bare footprints it leaves in the mud. In British Columbia, it is "Sasquatch", as the Salish natives call it. In the Salish language, the word means "hairy man" or "wild man". In other parts of the world, there are similar legends. In Asia, there is a legend of a large Abominable Snowman, or Yeti. It is described as over two metres tall and covered with long hair.

The Sasquatch has been described as having long arms and legs, with big hands and feet. It is over a metre and a half tall. Some people even claim to have photos of the animal. They are usually shot from a distance and are often hard to make out.

These stories and sightings have been around for many years. Some people propose that they are descendents of huge ape-like creatures from China. People suggest they crossed the Bering Strait around the same time that the first native people came. The Sasquatch could only survive by hiding in the day and coming out at night. As the land became developed, the Sasquatch was pushed into even more remote areas. The character appears in Indian myths and legends. Early explorers and hunters have reported sightings and the footprints have been found in the mud. But one supposed footprint brought in by Ray L. Wallace from California in 1958 is now known to be a hoax.

On October 20, 1967, Roger Patterson and Bob Gimlin travelled on horseback looking for the Big Foot in the Bluff Creek Riverbed in Northern California. Although they hoped to run into a Big Foot, they did not expect to actually see one. Suddenly the horses reared, bucking Patterson off. He then saw a large, hair-covered body by the river. Quickly he grabbed his 16mm camera and with only minutes left on his film, Patterson filmed as the animal stood up and began to walk away. He claimed to have the only film evidence ever gathered of a live Sasquatch. The film is shaky in the beginning, but becomes more stable toward the end when the animal can be seen and identified. In 2005, the Sasquatch again made the news because a piece of hair from the "monster" was found but unfortunately, scientists found out the hair was from a bison!

Making Inferences

In reading articles like this, you often make inferences or "read between the lines". This means that you have to use what you already know to evaluate what you are reading and see if it is true or logical.

A. Make inferences to write "T" for the true statements and "F" for the false ones.

1. _____ Rumours of a Sasquatch have existed for a very long time.

2. _____ Other cultures have similar stories of monsters that no one has ever been able to say for certain exist.

3. _____ Sightings of these animals usually occur in isolated areas where a second person cannot be asked to confirm the story.

4. _____ Scientists have been able to confirm the existence of a Sasquatch.

5. _____ Some people have faked evidence of the Sasquatch footprints.

6. _____ The sightings occur very regularly.

7. _____ The article gives evidence of people who are experts.

8. _____ There are Indian legends about the Sasquatch.

B. Answer the following questions.

1. The article implies that the Sasquatch is rarely seen because they avoid human contact. Copy a sentence from the passage which supports this statement.

_____

2. Why do you think Ray Wallace brought a plaster cast of the footprint and claimed it belonged to a Big Foot?

_____

3. Do you think the film Patterson shot should be accepted as evidence that the Big Foot exists?

_____

Framing Questions

Questions are useful in organizing our thoughts before writing or helping us get information from others. The six types of questions are: Who? What? Where? When? Why? How?

Imagine that you are going to interview the following two persons. Create a set of questions beforehand to get the most out of them.

Walter Gretzky

Avoid asking yes/no questions as you won't get much information.

Walter Gretzky is Wayne Gretzky's father. Walter was an avid hockey fan himself. He drilled Wayne on the basic skills and instilled in him the desire to practise hard and always give his all in every game. Walter actually turned their backyard into a rink in winter to let Wayne play and practise hockey.

When Wayne was just six years old, Walter managed to sign him to play with the ten-year-olds in the Atom League in Brantford, Ontario. Wayne was so small that his oversized hockey sweater constantly got in the way of his stick on his shooting side. So, he simply tucked in his jersey on the one side and years later, thousands of young hockey players would be wearing their jerseys the same way.

_____

_____

_____

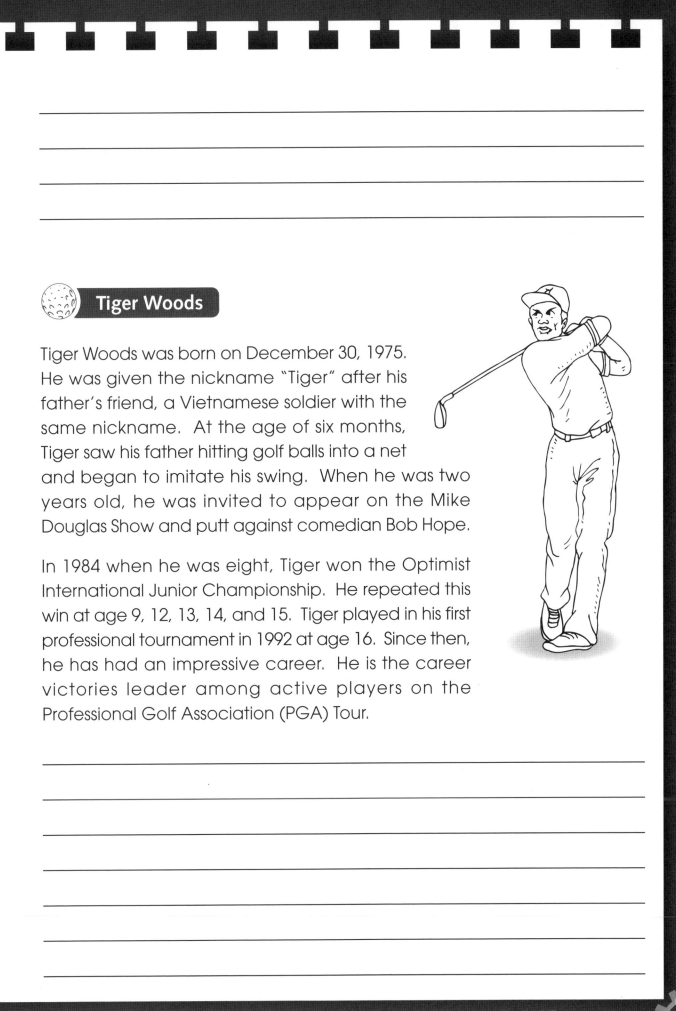

Tiger Woods

Tiger Woods was born on December 30, 1975. He was given the nickname "Tiger" after his father's friend, a Vietnamese soldier with the same nickname. At the age of six months, Tiger saw his father hitting golf balls into a net and began to imitate his swing. When he was two years old, he was invited to appear on the Mike Douglas Show and putt against comedian Bob Hope.

In 1984 when he was eight, Tiger won the Optimist International Junior Championship. He repeated this win at age 9, 12, 13, 14, and 15. Tiger played in his first professional tournament in 1992 at age 16. Since then, he has had an impressive career. He is the career victories leader among active players on the Professional Golf Association (PGA) Tour.

Canada's Youngest Territory

A new territory, Nunavut, was created from part of the Northwest Territories on April 1, 1999. It is twice the size of British Columbia and larger than any other territory or province.

Most of its residents are Inuit. The official languages are Inuktitut, Dene, English, and French. Nunavut means "our land" in Inuktitut. The new territory has a unique feature of government: there is an equal number of male and female members of the legislature. The government is called *consensus government*. There are no political parties like in the other provinces.

Eight Cabinet ministers and the premier are selected by the 24 members of the Legislative Assembly who run as independents during elections. That means they do not run for election as members of the various political parties in Canada – the Liberals, Conservatives, or New Democrats – but as individuals.

Most of the population of Nunavut is Aboriginal; 83% are Inuit. Earlier in history the Inuit developed the kayak, the igloo, the parka, and dog sled teams. Nunavut contains many proud communities such as Baffin Island with its sled dogs and caribou; Cape Dorset with its famous soapstone carvings; and Ellesmere Island, known for its seal fishing and its polar bears. These are just a few of the special places and things the territory has to offer.

To see examples of the Dene and Inuit native languages, go to www.gov.nu.ca. There are many beautiful pictures of Nunavut on the site, too.

Making notes on what you have read helps you to understand and organize information. It also helps to clarify your thinking.

Make point form notes on the information you have read to fill in the concept map below.

- Established: _____

- Main population group: _____

- Official languages: _____

  _____

- Location: _____

  _____

- Size: _____

  _____

Nunavut

Meaning:

Art:

_____

_____

Culture

Government

Activities:

_____

_____

Unique feature:

_____

_____

_____

_____

Did You Know?

Nunavut is a producer of some colourful gems such as amber and sapphire.

Day

35

Direct and Indirect Speech (1)

Direct speech repeats exact words spoken; these words are put in between quotation marks.

Example: Mrs. Martin said to Paul, "You can take one."

Indirect speech reports what someone else said; no quotation marks are needed.

Example: Mrs. Martin told Paul that he could take one.

Changing direct speech to indirect speech involves tense changes; the tense in indirect speech is one tense back in time from that in direct speech.

We don't need to change the tense if the reporting verb is in present tense, or if the statement is about something that is still true.

A. Change the following sentences to indirect speech.

1. Ivan says, "I always enjoy window-shopping with them."

   _____

   _____

2. "They have been working on the project," said Mr. Ross.

   _____

3. "I will attend the ceremony," said Fred's father.

   _____

4. Karen said, "I'm never good at singing."

   _____

5. Ted explained, "The moon revolves around the Earth."

   _____

6. "We've tried many ways," Evelyn said to Mrs. Wayne.

   _____

7. "I like the cotton dress more," said Mabel.

   _____

Direct Speech to Indirect Speech: Other Changes

Time Reference

In indirect speech, we need to change time reference.

Example: Dan said, "They will hold a garage sale <u>next week</u>."

Dan said that they would hold a garage sale <u>the following week</u>.

Personal Pronouns

We need to change personal pronouns to the third person singular or plural, except when the speakers reports his own words.

Example: Ms. Weir said to him, "<u>I</u> like what <u>you</u> did."

Ms. Weir told him that <u>she</u> liked what <u>he</u> had done.

B. **Change the following sentences to indirect speech using the time references provided.**

> the day before   two days later   the following week
> the week before   that day   a week before

1. "I didn't play in the game yesterday," said Alex to his father.

   _____

2. "It happened a week ago," said Ron.

   _____

3. "Grandma will come the day after tomorrow," said Molly.

   _____

4. The waiter said, "We serve fresh seafood today."

   _____

5. The teacher said, "Next week, there will be two new students in our class."

   _____

   _____

6. "They went to Hamilton last week," said Bill.

   _____

   _____

Could You Pass a Citizenship Test?

If you were born in Canada, you are automatically a Canadian citizen. But there are other ways you can become a citizen. The following conditions apply if you wish to become a citizen of Canada (children do not have to meet all of the requirements):

- you must be informed and complete a test about Canada's history, geography, and political system

- you must have lived in Canada for at least three years

- you must swear an oath of allegiance

- you must be 18 years or older

- you must speak French or English

A citizen has rights and responsibilities. When you are a citizen of Canada, you can participate actively in public life by voting, serving on juries, or running for an elected office. You also have an obligation to contribute in a meaningful way to your society and to obey the laws.

Canadian citizenship is younger than Canada itself. Canada became a nation on July 1, 1867 when the Fathers of Confederation met in Charlottetown, Prince Edward Island to join this nation. But when Canada became a Confederation, it remained a colony of the British Commonwealth, and its citizens carried British passports.

The Canadian Citizenship Act, which was passed on January 1, 1947, was drafted by Paul Martin Senior after he visited a Canadian cemetery in Dieppe, France. Martin Sr. observed that soldiers from a variety of backgrounds had fought and died as Canadian soldiers. He felt that Canadians should carry a Canadian passport, not a British one, as their badge of citizenship. For this reason, he drafted the motion which became law.

The following are some of the questions that would appear on a citizenship test. See if you could answer them correctly.

You may need to ask an adult, consult some reference books, or visit _www.citzine.ca_. It is a Web magazine developed by Citizenship and Immigration Canada to get people thinking about what it means to be citizens of this country.

1. What are the two official languages of Canada?

_____

2. What is the name of the Prime Minister of Canada?

_____

3. Who was the first prime minister of Canada?

_____

4. Where are the Parliament Buildings located?

_____

5. In what year did Canada become a country?

_____

6. How many provinces and territories are there in Canada?

_____

7. What are the three main groups of Aboriginal peoples?

_____

8. What are the names of the five Great Lakes?

_____

_____

_____

_____

_____

Did You Know?

The concept of citizenship goes all the way back to ancient Greece. In the Greek city-states, "citizens" were people who had special rights in society and in return, agreed to help run the community.

Direct and Indirect Speech (2)

Note the following when changing direct questions to indirect questions:
- The tense in indirect questions is one tense back in time from that in direct questions.
- There is no need to use "Do/Does/Did".
- Change "Yes/No" questions by using "ask if/whether...".

Example: One of the players asked, "Will I be sidelined?"
One of the players <u>asked if</u> he would be sidelined.

A. Change the following questions to indirect speech.

1. "Which is the one you want?" Mrs. Watson asked Ben.

    _____

    _____

2. They asked, "When can we start?"

    _____

3. "Did you come that way?" the police officer asked.

    _____

4. She asked him, "Are you going with me tomorrow?"

    _____

5. "Have you seen my cat?" Mrs. Healey asked her neighbour.

    _____

B. Change the following indirect statements to direct ones.

1. Margaret told me that she wanted to buy that bracelet.

    _____

2. The coach told the players that there would not be any games until the following Saturday.

    _____

3. The teacher said that it was a holiday the following day.

_____

4. The woman asked if they could take her to their school.

_____

5. Carol asked Bill if he had got an MP3 player.

_____

6. The delivery man asked if there was anyone in the house.

_____

C. Correct the following indirect statements.

1. The man said that he will let me know next week.

_____

2. I asked him if he has seen my Science book.

_____

3. The librarian asked did I borrow the storybook.

_____

4. I remarked that there were 29 days in February every four years.

_____

5. Wendy said that she has lived there for almost 10 years.

_____

D. Rewrite what Felix said in indirect speech.

We'll have a game with Harry's team tomorrow but we haven't quite prepared yet because a lot of my teammates are still busy with their projects and they do not have time for practice. I think we'll lose.

_____

_____

_____

The Mohawk Poet

E. Pauline Johnson was born on the Six Nations Iroquois Reserve, near Brantford, Ontario. Her mother was an English woman and her father a Mohawk chief. Her Aboriginal name was Tekahionwake. She lived from 1861 to 1913.

Pauline toured the United States, Canada, and England giving dramatic readings of her poetry. She appeared on stage in a buckskin dress, a dress made of deer hide. She also wore a beaded belt that showed the beautifully intricate work of native designs. Her poems are beautiful and she gained an international reputation. She was very proud of her native ancestry and her poems reflect her love of nature.

The following are two stanzas from her poem "The Pilot of the Plains", which demonstrates her use of rich language and her ability to create pictures with words. The poem is a story of a native girl and a white man who are married but separated. The young wife is waiting in the village for her husband's return.

"Till the autumn came and vanished, till the season of the rains,
Till the western world lay fettered in midwinter's crystal chains,
Still she listened for his coming,
Still she watched the distant plains."

Do you see the changing seasons and the image of a cold winter's day? Try to imagine yourself as one of the hunters, or as the maiden, when reading the final stanza:

"Late at night, say Indian hunters, when the starlight clouds or wanes,
Far away they see a maiden, misty as the autumn rains,
Guiding with her lamp of moonlight
Hunters lost upon the plains."

The Indian maid is a ghost who has become the "pilot of the plains". She has abandoned the warmth of her home to go into the winter night to look for her lost love, and is now a restless ghost guiding others to safety.

Poetry is a different style of writing, or "genre". **Genre** means "type of writing". The excerpts you have just read come from a narrative poem, one that tells a story.

Answer the following questions.

1. Can you fill in the missing parts of the poem from your imagination? Use five or six sentences to tell your own version of the story of the young couple. Explain how the wife becomes the "pilot of the plains".

   _____

   _____

   _____

   _____

   _____

2. What do you think E. Pauline Johnson means by the words "crystal chains"? Describe in your own words the image that you see in your mind when you read those words.

   _____

   _____

   _____

   _____

   _____

3. Paragraphs in poetry are called stanzas. Write the rhyming words for each stanza.

   _____

   _____

   _____

Did You Know?

The "E" in E. Pauline Johnson is the initial for "Emily".

Phrases

There are three types of **phrases**: adjective phrases, adverb phrases, and noun phrases.

An **adjective phrase** describes a noun.

Example: Boxes <u>made of wood</u> are durable.

An **adverb phrase** describes a verb.

Example: The soldiers marched <u>across the field</u>.

A **noun phrase** is made up of a noun and all its modifiers.

Example: They were locked up in <u>a small and stuffy room</u>.

A. Underline the noun phrase(s) in each of the following sentences.

1. I was shocked to see the fluffy, creepy thing.

2. The losing team put up a good fight to the end.

3. We were all exhausted after the long, uphill climb.

4. She always enjoys a cool, refreshing drink by the pool.

5. It was an extremely boring movie.

6. There are altogether seven honour students in our class.

7. Mother baked a delicious cheesecake for us.

8. The red, sleek sports car sped past me like an arrow.

9. We never expected such a warm and fun reception.

10. No one knew what that thick, oily substance was.

11. The long, bumpy ride lasted almost an hour.

12. He is the most skilful player we have ever met.

B. **Underline the adjective phrases and place parentheses around the adverb phrases in the following sentences.**

1. His dog managed to jump across the ditch.
2. The food in the cooler had gone bad.
3. All the guests waited in the hallway.
4. The members of the team were each given a name tag.
5. That afternoon, all the workers assembled in the compound.
6. No one from his group wanted to do the presentation.
7. The fugitive crawled through the tunnel and escaped.
8. The coach of the opposing team did not think it was fair.
9. Fred played video games from morning to night.
10. He climbed up the tall tree to save the cat.
11. The jellybeans were scattered all over the place.
12. The guards of the palace ordered them to leave.

C. **Write sentences that contain an adjective phrase, an adverb phrase, or a noun phrase. Underline the phrase in each of your sentences.**

Adjective Phrase

1. _____
2. _____

Adverb Phrase

1. _____
2. _____

Noun Phrase

1. _____
2. _____

Day
40

**Read the clues and complete
the crossword puzzle.**

Across

A.   a kind of shellfish

B.   a kind of Italian pasta

C.   a long animal with no legs

D.   a small, soft animal with a hard shell

E.   odour

F.   You can use glue to do this.

Down

1.   an animal that can send out an unpleasant smell

2.   clever

3.   how a snake moves

4.   sudden rush of a large group of animals

5.   the opposite of "swift"

6.   the opposite of "rough"

7.   a small desert animal with
     a poisonous sting in its tail

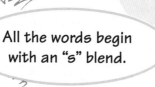

All the words begin
with an "s" blend.

Beothuks – Newfoundland's Native People

The Beothuks were the aboriginal people of the island of Newfoundland who are now extinct. Shanawdithit, the last known Beothuk, died in St. John's in 1829. Forensic scientists ask why the Beothuks died out completely. One reason is that they did not rely on fur trade to get the iron tools that the native people could not create. Unlike the Mi'kmaqs of the mainland, the Beothuks did not gather at fur trading posts to await the arrival of the ships that brought traders. Instead, they waited until the Europeans left the fishing station to scavenge for the metal goods they desired. But this also meant that they had to continue moving inland, away from the rich source of food the ocean provided, in order to avoid contact with the Europeans.

Around the middle of the 18th century, the Beothuks moved further inland to avoid contact with the English. As English settlement expanded, these pioneers to Newfoundland took the roles of either furriers or trappers and the Beothuks had to compete with the white Europeans for the animals. By the beginning of the 19th century, the Beothuks were reduced to a small refugee population living along the Exploits River system and Red Indian Lake attempting to exist on the resources of the interior. This was a very hard life because the climate and environment of Newfoundland do not support agriculture.

One of the last known Beothuk women is Demasduit, the wife of the Beothuk Chief. Their band was one of the last remaining ones in Newfoundland. Demasduit was abducted by the English settlers in St. John's. She painted and drew many scenes of her native life while in captivity. She was renamed Mary March by the white settlers. She died of tuberculosis.

Lady Hamilton, the wife of the governor of Newfoundland, painted a portrait of Demasduit in 1816. The portrait shows a delicate looking woman with wise, sad brown eyes and delicate features. Lady Hamilton wrote about the captive in her diary and said that she appeared to be an intelligent woman who was learning to speak English. While it appears that Lady Hamilton was kind to "Mary", she did not have any regard for the fact that this native woman would miss her baby who was left behind when she was captured.

A. **Read the clues and complete the crossword puzzle with words from the passage.**

Across

A. a kind of infectious disease
B. search among waste for things
C. people who sell furs
D. people who trap animals for their furs

Down

1. taken away by force
2. someone who is kept imprisoned
3. group of people
4. native

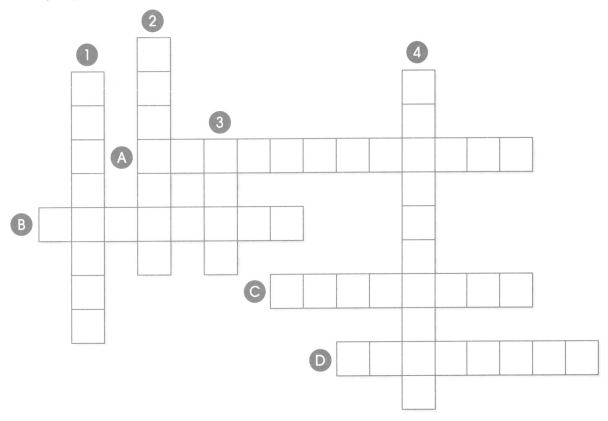

B. **Write the main idea of each paragraph in one or two sentences.**

Paragraph 1: _____

_____

Paragraph 2: _____

_____

Paragraph 3: _____

_____

Paragraph 4: _____

_____

Adjective and Adverb Phrases

Phrases

A **phrase** is a group of words that has no subject or predicate and is often introduced by a preposition. A preposition is a linking word between a noun or a pronoun and other words in a sentence.

Adjective phrases describe nouns.

Example: The tourists <u>on the boat</u> are amazed by the spectacular sight.

"On the boat" describes "the tourists".

Adverb phrases describe verbs.

Example: They finally arrived <u>in the evening</u>.

"In the evening" describes "arrived".

A. **Underline the phrase in each of the following sentences. Write "adj" for an adjective phrase and "adv" for an adverb phrase.**

1. The children were swimming in the pool. _____

2. The room was used for storing stationery and books. _____

3. The man on the bench is our coach. _____

4. She bought the skirt with a huge pink bow. _____

5. The book on the table is not mine. _____

6. The team only practised on weekends. _____

7. The kite with a long tail is mine. _____

8. The children from the daycare centre enjoyed the show. _____

9. All the mice sneaked into the hole. _____

10. The space shuttle touched down in the morning. _____

B. **Rewrite each of the following sentences by adding an adjective phrase.**

1. I like the puppy.

    _____

2. The woman is my aunt.

    _____

3. The backpack belongs to my sister.

    _____

4. The clowns bumped into one another.

    _____

5. The man did not allow us in.

    _____

6. Who is the man?

    _____

C. **Rewrite each of the following sentences by adding an adverb phrase.**

1. The hurricane blew.

    _____

2. All of us waited.

    _____

3. The grade six boys were practising.

    _____

4. One of the children stopped.

    _____

5. The sprinters dashed.

    _____

6. The car continued to skid.

    _____

UNESCO

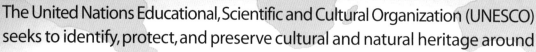

The United Nations Educational, Scientific and Cultural Organization (UNESCO) seeks to identify, protect, and preserve cultural and natural heritage around the world considered to be of outstanding value to humanity. Places as unique and diverse as the wilds of East Africa's Serengeti, the pyramids of Egypt, the Great Barrier Reef in Australia, and the Baroque cathedrals of Latin America make up our world's heritage. What makes the United Nations's concept of World Heritage exceptional is the belief that the sites belong to all the peoples of the world, regardless of the territory on which they are located.

Heritage is our legacy from the past, what we live with today, and what we pass on to future generations. Our cultural and natural heritage are both irreplaceable sources of life and inspiration. UNESCO's World Heritage mission is to:

- ensure the protection of natural and cultural heritage;
- encourage countries to nominate sites for inclusion on the World Heritage List;
- encourage establishment of management plans and set up reporting systems on the state of conservation of World Heritage sites;
- help safeguard World Heritage properties by providing technical assistance and professional training;
- provide emergency assistance for World Heritage sites in immediate danger;
- support public awareness-building activities for World Heritage conservation;
- encourage the preservation of a country's cultural and natural heritage;
- encourage international cooperation.

Canada has many places listed as World Heritage sites. Some are culturally significant, meaning that they tell the story of Canada's peoples. Head Smashed-in Buffalo Jump and L'Anse aux Meadows National Historic Site are two such sites.

Others are natural geological treasures, places of great beauty, or natural wonders. Examples of these are Dinosaur Provincial Park, Canadian Rocky Mountain Parks, and Waterton Glacier International Peace Park.

One way to learn new vocabulary is to read the words in context. This means locating the sentence where the word occurs and figuring out the meaning from its use in the sentence. We can usually get an idea of what the word means from the sentence.

A. Explain the following in your own words.

1. heritage _____

2. safeguard _____

3. unique _____

4. conservation _____

5. concept _____

6. international _____

7. assistance _____

8. irreplaceable _____

B. List five possible reasons a place can be declared a World Heritage site.

1. _____

2. _____

3. _____

4. _____

5. _____

C. Write a paragraph on why Niagara Falls should be declared a World Heritage site. State whether it is a natural or cultural site, what makes it unique, how it is different from other falls, and why it should be preserved.

_____

_____

_____

_____

Clauses

Clauses can be independent or dependent.

An **independent clause** can stand on its own as a sentence with complete meaning.

A **dependent clause** cannot stand on its own and needs an independent clause to make its meaning complete.

Example: While we were waiting for the bus, it started to rain.

(dependent clause)   (independent clause)

A. **Decide if the underlined clause in each of the following sentences is an independent or a dependent clause. Write "IND" for an independent clause and "D" for a dependent clause.**

1. Although it was late, <u>they continued to work on the project</u>.   _____

2. Wherever she goes, <u>she carried her doll with her</u>.   _____

3. <u>As I was going home</u>, I saw Beth's little cousin.   _____

4. <u>If she asked more politely</u>, I would agree to help.   _____

5. <u>They gave up</u> because there was too little time.   _____

6. <u>However hard they tried</u>, they would not make it.   _____

7. <u>I would definitely go with you</u> if I knew he was there.   _____

8. Because the weather was bad, <u>we cancelled the trip</u>.   _____

9. <u>If you want to succeed</u>, you must put in effort and persevere.   _____

10. When the results were announced, <u>the audience booed and yelled</u>.   _____

11. It was a pleasant journey <u>although we had to go without her</u>.   _____

12. <u>She walks her dog</u> when she has nothing better to do.

B. **Add a dependent clause to each of the following sentences. Write the new sentence on the line.**

1. His father was very pleased.

    _____

2. He did not show up.

    _____

3. There was an uproar.

    _____

4. She would not give in.

    _____

5. They took the shortcut.

    _____

6. I will make a deal with you.

    _____

C. **Add an independent clause to each of the following sentences.**

1. Whenever I am free, _____ .

2. As they were chatting, _____ .

3. If you think I was the one who did it, _____

    _____ .

4. Although the two of us have never met before, _____

    _____ .

5. _____

    _____

    wherever he goes.

6. _____

    _____

    because they lost their way.

Head Smashed-in Buffalo Jump

"Head Smashed-in Buffalo Jump" is located in Alberta and UNESCO has designated it a World Heritage Site. UNESCO names certain sites all over the world for their uniqueness and importance in defining the history of the peoples of the Earth.

Does the name give you a clue to what might have happened there? Beginning nearly 6000 years ago, the native people of the Northwest Plains used to trap and kill large numbers of buffalo. The cliffs are over 10 metres high and at the base there are 11 m of butchered bones and tools left over from the buffalo hunts of long ago. Try to imagine how long it would take for bones to pile up 11 m high.

The buffalo hunt was an important way of life for the native people. It provided the food, tools, clothing, and ceremonial objects for the tribe. Native peoples relied on the land for food. They were very inventive when it came to trapping. 6000 years ago, the native people had only handmade wood spears and tools to trap and butcher the buffalo. Sometimes the native hunters would wear wolf skins or bawl like a buffalo calf to trick the buffalo into running over the cliff. The hunters would cooperate to get the herd stampeding. Then they would steer them in the direction of the cliff. Once the buffalo started running they would follow one another over the cliff. The cliff was called the "buffalo jump". Hunters would be waiting below the cliff to butcher the animals. The whole tribe would share in the kill and the tribe would have enough food and clothing for the long winter months.

Native people used all parts of the buffalo. The hair was used for padding and ornaments. The horns were used for cups, spoons, ornaments, and powder horns. The bones were used for knives or ornaments. The hide was used for clothing, containers, and covering for their homes. The tail was used in ceremonial activities. The hooves were used for rattles and glue, and the marrow was used to make soup. The meat was roasted, boiled, or dried. Even the skull was used in ceremonial dances.

Visualization

One of the techniques for remembering information is **visualization**. Close your eyes and picture the cliff and the herd of buffalo. Picture them running over the cliff and what would happen next. Add as many details as you can in your mind.

A. Using the picture you have created in your mind, write a paragraph about the "buffalo jump" with as many details as possible.

_____

_____

_____

_____

B. Make a concept web of the uses the native people had for buffalo. Use headings such as food, clothing, etc. Then list the parts of the buffalo that were used for each purpose.

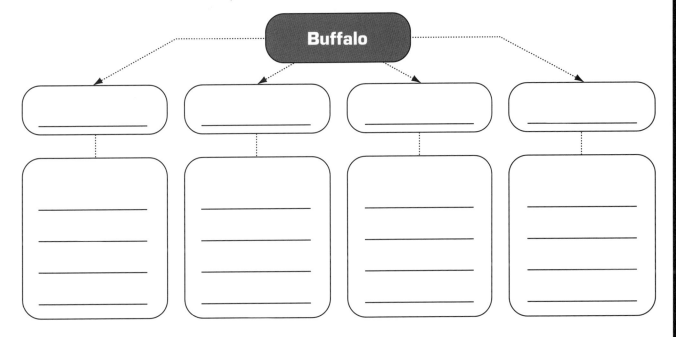

Why do you think the site is called "Head Smashed-in"? Who do you think named it?

_____

_____

Compound and Complex Sentences

A **compound sentence** is made up of two or more independent clauses connected by conjunctions.

Example: We looked up the sky and there were countless stars.

A **complex sentence** is made up of an independent clause with at least one dependent clause. A dependent clause is one that is not complete in meaning and has to depend on another clause to make the meaning complete.

Example: Although it was raining, the game continued.
          (dependent clause)   (independent clause)

A. **Add an independent clause to each of the following sentences to make it a compound sentence.**

1. It was a sunny day and _____ .

2. They arrived there ten minutes early but _____
_____ .

3. We can start all over again or _____
_____ .

4. The waitress did not say a word and _____
_____ .

5. The players were disgruntled but _____
_____ .

B. **Add a dependent or an independent clause to each of the following sentences to make it a complex sentence.**

1. We were told to stay indoor _____
_____ .

2. Although no one won the bonus prize, _____
_____ .

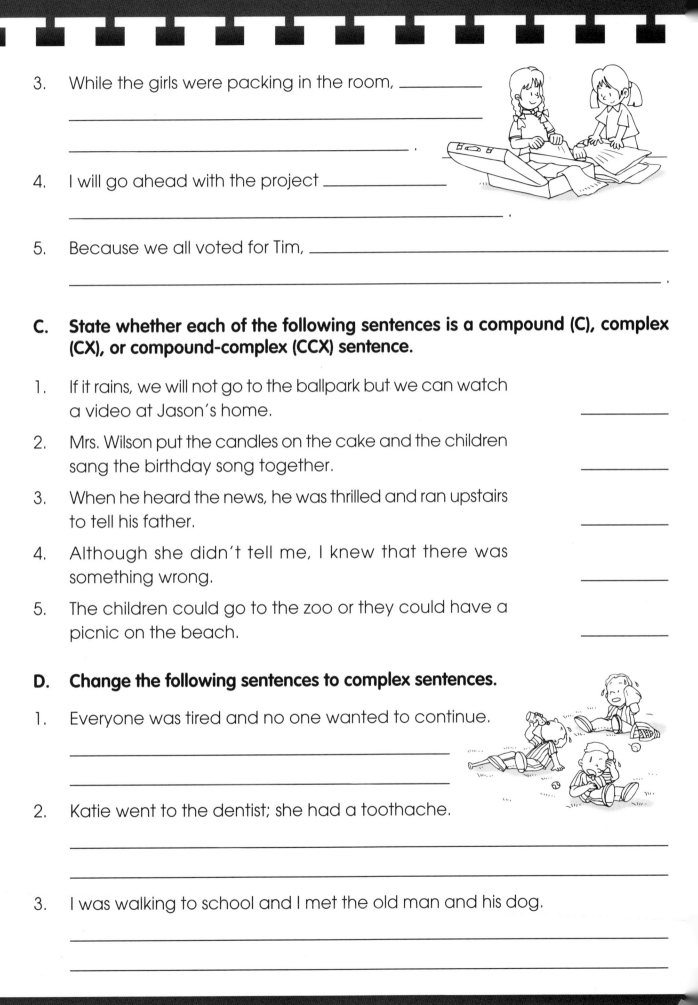

3. While the girls were packing in the room, _____

_____

_____ .

4. I will go ahead with the project _____

_____ .

5. Because we all voted for Tim, _____

_____ .

C. State whether each of the following sentences is a compound (C), complex (CX), or compound-complex (CCX) sentence.

1. If it rains, we will not go to the ballpark but we can watch a video at Jason's home. _____

2. Mrs. Wilson put the candles on the cake and the children sang the birthday song together. _____

3. When he heard the news, he was thrilled and ran upstairs to tell his father. _____

4. Although she didn't tell me, I knew that there was something wrong. _____

5. The children could go to the zoo or they could have a picnic on the beach. _____

D. Change the following sentences to complex sentences.

1. Everyone was tired and no one wanted to continue.

_____

_____

2. Katie went to the dentist; she had a toothache.

_____

_____

3. I was walking to school and I met the old man and his dog.

_____

_____

Date : _____

L'Anse aux Meadows – a UNESCO World Heritage Site
The earliest known European settlement in the New World

Five centuries before Columbus, the Vikings came to Canada. Ancient Norse stories had been told by word of mouth for many years and people in Canada knew there were rumours that Vikings had landed somewhere on Canada's coast. You may have heard of Erik the Red and his son Lief Eriksson, both famous Viking explorers. The stories the Vikings told are called sagas – tales of daring, courage, and adventure. According to these sagas, Lief and his crew of about 30 men set sail in a very large vessel with a square sail in search of new land. They travelled from Greenland.

People had been exploring Canada to see if they could find evidence to support the claim that Vikings had come to Canada and settled here for a while. Imagine the excitement in the archaeological community when the site was found in 1960 in the northern part of Newfoundland! It was excavated for eight years and then opened to the public. The settlement has been recreated and is very exciting to visit.

Declared a UNESCO World Heritage Site in 1978, the site at L'Anse aux Meadows consists of three Norse buildings reconstructed in the exact pattern found by archaeologists. Exhibits, with guides dressed in period costumes, interpret the highlights of the Viking lifestyle, artefacts, and the discovery of the site. The guides stay in character and you feel like you are really talking to a Viking from 1000 years ago! The grass-covered buildings have walls five feet thick and were both cool in summer and warm in winter. The Vikings built without trees because there are no trees in Greenland. You also get to visit a recreation of the vessel the Vikings used to sail to the New World.

It is not known how long the Vikings remained at the settlement in the New World. They stayed long enough to build several houses, workshops, and a small forge where they made things out of iron. The site was situated near a peat bog, which gave the Vikings a source of fuel for cooking, heating, and working in the forge.

Tips for Making Notes

Webs are one way of organizing information to help you read later and to summarize your ideas.

A. Make a zigzag web of ideas from the passage by filling in information under each heading.

Vikings came to North America

Exploration

Settlement

Discovery

UNESCO Site

B. Create a short report on what you have read by using the ideas in (A).

_____

_____

_____

_____

_____

_____

Day
48

Building Vocabulary

Root Words

A **root word** is the basic word from which other words are derived.

Example: agree (root word)
disagree (antonym)
agreeable (adjective)
agreement (noun)

A.   Build derivative words from the following root words.

1.   able   (antonym) _____   (noun)   _____

2.   tolerate   (adjective) _____   (noun)   _____

3.   quick   (verb)   _____   (adverb)   _____

4.   fertile   (antonym) _____   (noun)   _____

5.   formal   (antonym) _____   (noun)   _____

6.   successful   (antonym) _____   (noun)   _____

B.   Identify the root word for each of the following words.   Write it on the line provided.

1. discovery   _____   2.   seemingly   _____

3. division   _____   4.   probability   _____

5. monumental   _____

6. adventurous   _____

7. activity   _____

8. extraordinarily _____

9. unsatisfactorily _____

10. sportsmanship   _____

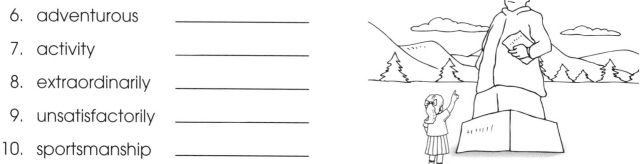

Prefixes

We can form new words by adding **prefixes** to them. These are some common prefixes:

in, im, un, anti, dis – opposites
pro – in favour of; for
out – better than, greater than, separate from
mis – wrong
pre – before; at a previous time
hyper – more than usual
sub – below

C. Use the prefixes above to make new words.

1. active _____ : too active
2. smart _____ : be smarter than
3. government _____ : against the government
4. calculate _____ : calculate wrongly
5. dawn _____ : before dawn
6. possible _____ : not possible
7. understand _____ : understand wrongly
8. satisfied _____ : not satisfied
9. merged _____ : went below
10. fit _____ : not fit

Can you make five derivative words from these two root words?

11. help _____

12. true _____

Date : _____

Rock My World!

Some features of the Canadian National Park at Gros Morne in Newfoundland are so unusual that they are nationally and internationally famous. Geologists from around the world visit Gros Morne to study its fossils and to learn about the history of the world from the formations of its ancient rocks.

The park is a wild landscape of fjords, seacoast, forests, and mountains, but it is the rocks that make it famous. UNESCO declared the park a World Heritage site in 1987, and it is permanently protected by the Government of Canada.

The two geographical components of Newfoundland – Labrador and the island of Newfoundland – are divided by the Strait of Belle Isle. These two places have the most interesting and oldest rocks found in Canada.

The Earth is composed of several large plates that cover the planet like a giant jigsaw puzzle. When the puzzle "shifts", the plates fold over or under one another. If the push is big enough, the plates are heaved up into a pile. Most earthquakes are caused when plates push against one another. This is one way that mountains and valleys are formed.

In fact, Labrador came about 400 million years ago when different areas of the world were brought together by the constant movement of plates on the Earth's surface – called continental drift. As the easternmost part of the Canadian Shield, Labrador is made up mostly of plutonic and metamorphic rocks, which are among the oldest rocks known on Earth.

It is due also to continental drift that the land and rocks of central Newfoundland are the remains of an ocean floor that once lay between North America and Africa. This was 500 million years ago, when the west coast of Africa was part of the margin of North America.

Concept Words

When you read a passage, there are **concept words** which are important for you to understand in order to get information from the text.

A. Match the following concept words with their meanings.

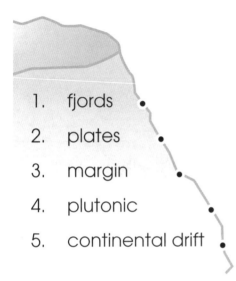

1. fjords
2. plates
3. margin
4. plutonic
5. continental drift

- A the edge of the land mass
- B rocks formed from molten lava
- C movement of the plates on the Earth's surface
- D long narrow bodies of water with extremely high rocky banks
- E areas of different sizes and shapes moving about the surface of the planet

B. Answer the following questions.

1. If you were a geologist, what would you study? Why?

_____

_____

2. Describe the wild landscape of Gros Morne.

_____

3. Why would Gros Morne be the perfect place to learn about the formation of the continent?

_____

_____

_____

Did You Know?

The name "Gros Morne" is of French origin – *gros* means "big" and *morne* is a Creole word for "rounded mountain standing alone".

Day **50**

You Deserve A Break!

Put the words in order and write the names of these famous stories.

1. the   Jack   Beanstalk   and

   _____

2. The   New   Emperor's   Suit

   _____

3. Three   Goldilocks   Bears   the   and

   _____

4. Wizard   The   Oz   of

   _____

5. Factory   the   Charlie   and   Chocolate

   _____

6. Riding   Red   Hood   Little

   _____

7. Gretel   Hansel   and

   _____

8. The   Match-Seller   Little

   _____

9. Beast   and   Beauty   the

   _____

10. in   Wonderland   Alice

   _____

Choose three stories and design a book cover for each one.

Homophone Challenge

Homophones

Homophones are words that sound alike but have different spellings and meanings. These words are often confused when we create sentences.
Example: She couldn't <u>bear</u> to see the wounded kitten suffer. (✔)
　　　　　She couldn't <u>bare</u> to see the wounded kitten suffer. (✘)

A. Underline the word that suits the meaning of the sentence in each of the following sentences.

1.　The houseboat was on (sale / sail) for a good price.

2.　He could not (brake / break) in time and his bike slammed into the wall.

3.　I don't think this puppy is (theirs / there's).

4.　Do you like eating (muscles / mussels)?

5.　The (stares / stairs) of the crowd made the rookie pitcher nervous.

6.　It was so noisy that I simply couldn't (hear / here) what she was telling me.

7.　He helped his teacher (pour / pore) the liquid into the test tube.

8.　She wanted to find out (whether / weather) or not the bag was hers.

B. Use the clues to find the homophone pairs.

1.　a dog's feet

　　stop for a moment

2.　fuzzy leather

　　moved back and forth

3.　what you did with a book

　　a bright colour

4. an odour _____

   a coin _____

5. a type of blue pants _____

   biological molecules _____

6. a day of the week _____

   ice cream treat _____

7. a big animal _____

   without clothing _____

C. **Read the clues and complete the crossword puzzle with homophones of the words in parentheses.**

Across

A. large branch (bow)

B. head of a school (principle)

C. amazing act (feet)

D. given by the sun (raise)

Down

1. part of your body (waste)

2. rooms (sweets)

3. person who pays for food and lodgings (border)

4. differ (very)

The First Maps

Boy, I certainly looked different back then.

1205

2005

Exhibit 12

Have you ever studied a map of the world? How about one showing boundaries of the countries in medieval times? They look pretty different, don't they?

If you look at a medieval map of the world for the first time, you might wonder what the map maker was thinking. You would probably wonder where some of the continents were – such as the North and South Americas, and Australia – as well as many other places that you would expect to see. You might also wonder why Africa was right next to Europe, instead of below it. You would wonder why the map did not have a North and a South Pole, and why there was a large section called "the unknown".

People did not have the time or money to be as curious about the world as we are today, especially in Europe. They thought, "I have everything I need here, so why would I want to know what's over there?"

It was quite some time before people even accepted that the world was not flat.

Most people who lived in Europe thought that the answer to any and every question could be found in the Bible. Since the Bible often mentioned the four corners of the Earth, people just assumed then that the world was square and flat. People who sailed too far out into the ocean would eventually sail right off the edge of the world!

Most world maps at the time were very decorative, and could not be used to find places. Map makers were more interested in drawing maps that looked nice, rather than maps that actually showed where places were. Because many map makers thought the oceans looked too boring, they often created islands where there was none, and drew scary sea monsters rising from the depths.

Could you imagine if map makers still did that today?

Answer the following questions.

1. What would a medieval world map have looked like? Draw a version of it based on what you have read in the passage.

2. If most of the medieval maps could not be used to find places, why do you think people made them?

_____

_____

3. Aside from geographers, which group or groups of professionals do you think would be especially interested in maps during the first decades of the 20th century? Explain your answer.

_____

_____

Challenge

If you were a map maker in 1300, how would you go about making a map of Europe? Think about what you would do, who you would consult, and where you would go.

_____

_____

_____

_____

Synonyms and Antonyms

A **synonym** is a word that means the same as another word.
Example: lofty – high

An **antonym** is a word that is opposite in meaning to another word.
Example: simple – sophisticated

A. **Read the following sentences. Suggest a synonym for each of the words in parentheses.**

1. Aaron is an (ardent) _____ fan of the Edmonton Oilers.

2. His (precise) _____ directions helped us find the right way to the museum.

3. My mother was (delighted) _____ to go to their anniversary party.

4. He was so (agile) _____ that the two defencemen were unable to block him.

5. It was a (grave) _____ mistake that Matt had made.

6. I think this is a (touchy) _____ issue that is best left for the manager to decide.

7. The doctor's (prognosis) _____ was that she would (recover) _____ in about a month.

8. The scientist (analysed) _____ the (specimen) _____ to determine its (classification) _____ .

9. The (mammoth) _____ polar bear (slumbered) _____ in the warm sunshine.

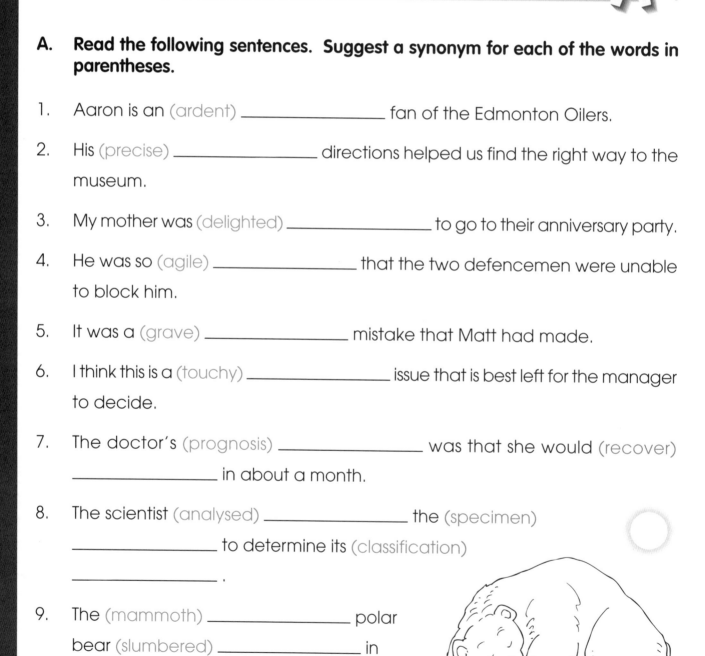

B. **Read the clue words and complete these antonym crossword puzzles.**

1. **Across** A. compact
   B. rough

   Down gain

2. **Across** A. downtown
   B. expand

   Down vacant

   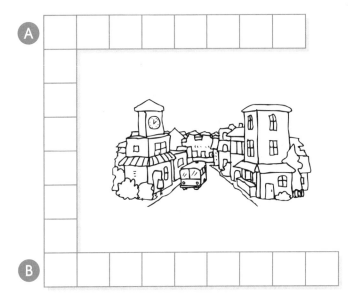

3. **Across** A. sluggish
   B. murky

   Down common

4. **Across** A. slow
   B. foolish

   Down initial

   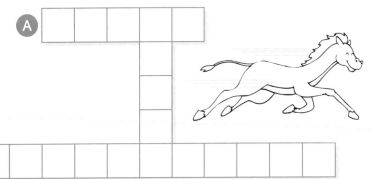

Date : _____

Marco Polo – a Medieval Explorer

Venice, Italy is located very strategically on the ocean with easy trading access to many places. The city became a major trading hub for lands in the West to trade with lands in the East in the 13th century. The Polo family was a merchant family from Venice, and Marco Polo was their famous son. He travelled to China to collect goods to bring back to Venice to sell. His journeys lasted 24 years, from 1271 to 1295.

It was a remarkable journey at the time. Marco Polo sailed from Venice and reached Greece or Constantinople – what is Turkey today. But when he left his ship, the only means of transportation available to him was horse, donkey, elephant, or on foot! He crossed deserts, mountains, and plains, went into areas occupied by the warlords of China, down the Pacific coast, around India, through what are now Iran and Iraq, and back to Venice. His explorations took him to many nations where he could not speak the language. Marco wrote a book about his travels, but his experiences were so different from what medieval people knew of the world that many thought he made up the tales.

Marco Polo opened up what became known as "The Silk Route". It extended from China to what is now Istanbul. If the Europeans wanted to trade for Asian goods, they first had to travel across the Mediterranean Sea, and cross large tracts of land through the Muslim nations that controlled the Silk Route and the spices people wanted for their food.

The Venetian explorer's descriptions inspired Columbus two centuries later to look for a route to China and the rich spice trade. It took too long to go overland through Asia, so Columbus set out in his ship to find another passage. What he discovered instead was North America!

A. Write "T" for the true statements and "F" for the false ones.

1. The Silk Route extended from China to Iraq. _____

2. Marco Polo travelled to China by sea. _____

3. People did not believe what Marco Polo wrote about his travels. _____

4. The Silk Route was controlled by the Muslim nations. _____

5. Columbus intended to travel to North America. _____

6. Marco Polo spoke many languages, which helped him communicate with the various peoples he met in his travels. _____

7. Marco Polo started his trip to China when he turned 24. _____

8. There was a rich spice trade at the time of Columbus. _____

B. Match these words with their meanings by writing the correct letters on the lines.

1. strategically _____   A. route

2. remarkable _____   B. stretches of land

3. explorations _____   C. exceptional

4. medieval _____   D. journeys of discoveries

5. passage _____   E. in a tactical way

6. tracts _____   F. relating to the Middle Ages

Challenge

Write a short paragraph explaining why Marco Polo was a remarkable medieval explorer.

_____

_____

_____

_____

Day

55

Mixing up Words

We may take one word for another because:

– the two words sound almost the same.

Example: Who's bag is that? (✘)

Whose bag is that? (✔)

– they look similar.

Example: The school adapts a new attendance system. (✘)

The school adopts a new attendance system. (✔)

– their meanings are related.

Example: His words had no affect on her. (✘)

His words had no effect on her. (✔)

A. **Choose the correct word to complete each of the following sentences.**

1. accept / except

a. Everyone came to the party _____ Valerie.

b. They will readily _____ any offer you put forth.

2. advice / advise

a. Please _____ me when I should arrive for the rehearsal.

b. The teacher gave him a good piece of _____ .

3. imminent / eminent

a. His departure is _____ , especially with the recent blunder he's made.

b. Her father is an _____ professor in the field of bio-engineering.

4. childish / childlike

a. His creativity is due a large extent to his _____ curiosity.

b. We are put off by his _____ behaviour.

5. respectful / respectable

a. Beth is always _____ to her teachers.

b. Mr. Diaz is a _____ teacher whom everyone likes.

B. Replace the underlined word with one that is more appropriate in meaning in each of the following sentences.

1. "Can we swim in the pool?" asked the little children. _____

2. I think Keith and Corey were involved, beside Simon. _____

3. Carl won't act foolishly; after all, he is a sensitive person. _____

4. We are waiting anxiously to meet the players. _____

5. Like I said, he would do whatever you asked him. _____

6. The robbery was committed last night when they were not at home. _____

C. Write sentences to show the difference in meaning between each pair of words.

1. take / bring

_____

_____

2. borrow / lend

_____

_____

3. serve / service

_____

_____

Racing to the Finish Line?

The mid-June day of the final track and field meet was met by temperatures approaching 30°C. The air was still and the scorching sun blazed down on the competitors who huddled under the sparse trees for shade. They were consuming bottle after bottle of water to keep the heat down.

Lisa, an 11-year-old runner, was the one hope her school had of bringing home a ribbon. She excelled in the 200-metre race, which demanded endurance and strategy. Small in size, she was big in heart, and her legs were like pistons pumping fiercely when she ran. Lisa had placed first in the divisional race and second in the regional where she was defeated by a mere two seconds by her main competitor, another 11-year-old runner named Jennifer. Jennifer was a tall girl with long legs that enabled her to run in steady, loping strides. Both runners were fierce competitors and superb athletes. Both were determined to win.

The announcement came for the 200-metre final. Runners were asked to report to the starter. There was already a swell of spectators at the finish line. Lisa and Jennifer set themselves into the starting blocks, focused straight ahead. They arched their backs and lowered their heads. The starter raised the pistol, and at the sound of the shot, they were off. The championship race was on.

About 30 metres into the race, Lisa and Jennifer had both jumped out to an insurmountable lead over the rest, who were now racing for third place. Everyone watched the leading pair of runners run around the first turn and speed down the straight way. The crowd cheered wildly. At the 100-metre mark, Lisa had taken a slight lead, but Jennifer stayed just off her left shoulder waiting to make her move.

At 160 metres, the runners were again neck and neck, well ahead of the pack. Lisa then soared into the lead. But as she sprinted ahead, she stumbled and sprawled to the ground…

Irony

The story you have just read uses the technique of **irony**. In writing, irony is the development of events that is the opposite of what is expected. It can make the writing more interesting to the reader because it makes them think harder about what may happen next.

Answer the following questions.

1. What is the ironic twist in the story?

    _____

    _____

2. Why do you think there is a question mark in the title of the story?

    _____

3. Is there any hint throughout the story that there would be an ironic twist? If so, identify and explain it.

    _____

    _____

4. How do you think the rest of the story will unfold? Write your own ending.

    _____

    _____

    _____

    _____

    _____

    _____

    _____

Did You Know?

When irony occurs in a play where the audience knows what the characters are not aware of, it is called "dramatic irony".

Tricky Usage

The following are some cases of tricky usage that frequently cause confusion. Read the explanations and complete the sentences with the correct choices.

1. **among** and **between**

    "Among" refers to more than two people or things whereas "between" refers to two people or things.

    a. _____ the three new players, he is probably the most skilful.

    b. When you stand _____ the two basketball players, you look small.

    c. The six children wanted to share the candies equally _____ themselves.

2. **each other** and **one another**

    "Each other" refers to two people and "one another" refers to more than two.

    a. The twins always support _____ .

    b. The rowdy crowd yelled at _____ .

    c. I think you and I are best friends and should help _____ .

3. **fewer** and **less**

    "Fewer" refers to units and "less" refers to quantity.

    a. There were _____ people at the ceremony than I thought.

    b. You should eat _____ fatty food to stay healthy.

    c. He knew much _____ than I first thought.

4.   **lie** and **lay**

"Lie" means to rest in a certain position while "lay" means to place something.

a.   _____ down on the couch if you're tired.

b.   The librarian asked us to _____ the storybooks on the table.

c.   You shouldn't _____ in the afternoon sun.

5.   **in** and **into**

"In" means inside whereas "into" shows the movement from outside to inside.

a.   The woman walked straight _____ the manager's office.

b.   They moved _____ a much bigger house.

c.   Derek and I live _____ the same neighbourhood.

6.   **sit** and **set**

"Sit" means to take a seat and "set" means to place something somewhere.

a.   The teacher told him to _____ still.

b.   I helped _____ the table for dinner.

c.   Mr. Wakefield was invited to _____ next to the host.

7.   **it's** and **its**

"It's" is the contracted form for "it is" whereas "its" is a possessive adjective.

a.   I don't think _____ a smart dog.

b.   My dog keeps wagging _____ tail.

c.   No one knew _____ whereabouts.

Mars

For a long time many people believed that there was life on Mars. Although scientists tell us there is no life on Mars today, we have learned a lot of neat things about Mars over the years.

Did you know that a day on Mars is actually 37 minutes longer than it is here on Earth? That's because it takes 24 hours and 37 minutes for Mars to rotate on its axis once. By contrast, the Earth does it in just 24 hours. To understand what it means for something to spin on its axis, think of an orange with a stick poked through the centre. Put a dot on the orange to represent the place on Earth where you live. Now hold the orange by the stick and rotate the dot once in front of a light bulb, which represents the sun. You have just recreated a day on the planet. The part of the planet facing the light has day, and the part that is turned away from it experiences night. It takes Mars nearly two years to complete its orbit around the sun. That is what gives it the seasons. Winter is long and cold on Mars!

Scientists learn about Mars with the help of small robotic vehicles controlled from the Earth, called "rovers". These rovers have cameras attached to them, which are used to send pictures of Mars back to our planet. Scientists now believe, based on discoveries made by these rovers as well as satellites, that there are still active volcanoes on Mars.

Scientists have also discovered evidence to suggest that there may be water on Mars, or at least that it is capable of sustaining water. The rovers have taken pictures of clouds that appear to be water in gas form. They have also found a type of rock called goethite, which is quite common on Earth, but forms only in the presence of water.

These are really important discoveries because water is necessary to maintain life. This means that someday humans may be able to live on the Red Planet. Although there is no life on Mars today, it doesn't mean that there isn't life elsewhere in our galaxy. Do you think there is life somewhere in outer space, or do you think we are really alone?

A. Answer the following questions.

1. Why is winter on Mars longer than that on Earth?

   _____

2. What does the discovery of goethite on Mars suggest?

   _____

3. Why do you think scientists need to rely on rovers to collect data on Mars?

   _____

4. Why does the writer think that someday humans can live on Mars?

   _____

B. Read the clues and complete the crossword puzzle with words from the passage.

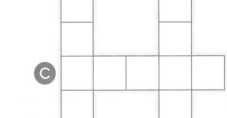

Across

A. system of billions of stars

B. sign that helps in making a conclusion or judgment

C. path along which a body revolves around another

D. straight line about which a planet rotates

Down

1. the opposite of "dormant"

2. openings on the surface of a planet

3. rotate, turn

Frequently Confused Words

We may confuse words that have similar spelling or sound alike. Using a dictionary to clarify the meaning is a useful way of ensuring that you are using the proper word.

> Is this a stationary or stationery item?

A. Choose the correct word for each of the following sentences.

1. Mariam received a lot of (presence, presents) _____ for her birthday.

2. She looks more elegant (than, then) _____ her elder sister.

3. The (patients, patience) _____ were all waiting patiently in Dr. Freeman's office.

4. The (principal, principle) _____ did not accept his explanation.

5. (Its, It's) _____ been quite some time since we last visited her.

6. He came (forth, fourth) _____ in the 400-metre race.

7. It seems that (theirs, there's) _____ is more durable than ours.

8. They walked carefully (thorough, through) _____ the narrow tunnel.

9. Please put the (waste, waist) _____ into the garbage can for me.

10. I think his business (fares, fairs) _____ well in the summer months.

11. Don't (accept, except) _____ anything from someone you don't know.

12. The view from the hilltop was indeed a splendid (site, sight) _____ .

13. She was exercising on her (stationery, stationary) _____ bicycle.

14. He was not (conscience, conscious) _____ after the accident.

15. They walked (passed, past) _____ the bag without noticing it.

B. Underline the misused word(s) in each of the following sentences. Write the correct word on the line.

1. The drought will effect the crop this year.

   _____

2. Luckily, they all suffered from miner injuries.

   _____

3. You should advice him not to do it anymore.

   _____

4. I don't quiet understand why he keeps doing it.

   _____

5. The children have completed their assignments all ready.

   _____

C. Write sentences to show the difference in meaning between each pair of words.

1. dairy   diary

   _____

   _____

2. Who's   Whose

   _____

   _____

3. loose   lose

   _____

   _____

You Deserve A Break!

Unscramble the words and write the names of the chocolate treats.

1. a r e w f
_____

2. a b r
_____

3. g u f e d
_____

4. r i o e b n w
_____

5. d e u n a s
_____

6. k a c e
_____

7. u o f d e n
_____

8. s o m s u e
_____

9. p y t s a r
_____

10. a f t p r i a
_____

11. t l e u r f f
_____

12. i c p l p o s e
_____

New CHOCOL

> Circle the chocolate treats in the word search.

```
                                              i
                                      h   e   d
                                  a   o   g   f
f  z  d  q  n  c  b  l  q  c  p  d  z  a
q  w  a  f  e  r  q  r  e  w  t  i  m  j
j  m  h  c  a  j  z  a  o  b  n  t  f  h
n  b  s  p  h  e  d  h  v  w  u  g  u  o
a  l  p  m  o  u  s  s  e  w  n  m  d  c
g  o  c  n  g  p  c  i  y  h  p  i  g  b
i  p  g  a  p  a  s  t  r  y  l  r  e  q
b  a  h  y  b  j  e  i  w  g  x  a  i  k
k  r  d  r  q  f  y  l  c  v  n  w  s  a
e  f  i  b  t  o  b  k  s  l  p  g  u  h
c  a  k  e  m  n  z  n  e  h  e  c  n  b
f  i  y  f  p  d  l  b  o  e  f  y  d  k
m  t  o  a  g  u  c  a  d  j  q  m  a  e
d  l  d  o  e  e  t  r  u  f  f  l  e  i
j  b  m  i  f  a  k  b  p  q  i  d  b  f
```

How Many Are There?

No one knows for sure how many species there are on the planet. Scientists are discovering new forms of life all the time. The Earth is home to a huge variety of living things. Think of what you see when you are outside – grass, trees, bugs, birds, raccoons, squirrels, and fish. All are living things. To make sense of this, people sort living things into different groups, or classifications.

How do scientists tell one group from another? They examine and classify. Size, shape, and colour are some characteristics that may be used to classify different things.

Living things are called organisms. Organisms which can be grouped together by the way they look, what they need to survive, and what makes them different from other living things, are classified into groups such as class, family, and species.

Think of your pet cats or dogs. They are warm-blooded, breathe air, and give birth to live young. They are classified as the same class – mammals. There are many families of animals that fall under the mammalian class, such as bears, giraffes, monkeys, and humans. Within each family may be different species. For instance, there is only one species of humans – *Homo sapiens* – but there are 36 different species of wild cats in the cat family. Some examples are the jungle cat, the black-footed cat, the cheetah, and the Canadian lynx. Despite the variety of species, all mammals share key characteristics such as breathing air and giving live birth. They do not lay eggs or breathe in water.

Do you know whether a whale is a mammal or a fish? It lives in water but gives birth to live young, comes to the surface to breathe air, and feeds its young milk from mammary glands. If you guessed mammal, you would be right. Scientists try to identify certain key characteristics from all of the observations made about living things to sort them into different groups.

Answer the following questions.

1. What are some characteristics that scientists use to classify things?

   _____

2. Name three species of wild cats.

   _____

3. What is the word that means having a body temperature well above that of the environment?

   _____

4. What key characteristics enable scientists to classify whales as mammals?

   _____

   _____

5. Why do you think it is important to classify living things?

   _____

   _____

Challenge

A difficulty with knowing exactly how many species exist is that some habitats are unexplored. Think carefully about places that are hard to get to. Then name some habitats that you think might not have been fully explored, and explain why.

_____

_____

_____

_____

_____

_____

Did You Know?

Spiders are not insects because unlike insects, they have eight legs and only two body segments. All insects must have three pairs of legs and three body segments.

Day
62

Faulty Sentence Construction

Faulty Parallels

A **faulty parallel** occurs when the coordinate elements in a sentence do not have a consistent grammatical construction.

Example: We like swimming, fishing, and baseball in the summer. (✘)
We like swimming, fishing, and playing baseball in the summer. (✔)

A. **Rewrite the following sentences to correct the faulty parallels.**

1. My sister always wants to get the lead role and becoming famous.

   _____

   _____

2. Weight gain is often the result of eating too much candy, junk food and eating between meals.

   _____

   _____

3. It is important to work hard and doing well in school.

   _____

   _____

4. They think science projects are more interesting than English.

   _____

   _____

5. Her success was due to her perseverance, hard work, and she was getting support from her family.

   _____

   _____

   _____

Dangling Modifiers

To avoid confusion in meaning, we need to keep the modifier close to the words it modifies.

Example: He saw an old building walking into an alley. (✘)

(The sentence seems to say that an old building was walking into an alley.)

Walking into an alley, he saw an old building. (✔)

B. **Rewrite the following sentences to correct the dangling and misplaced modifiers.**

You may change the order of the words or add new words.

1. They specially baked a huge birthday cake for her.

_____

_____

2. The undercover police officer caught the pickpocket posing as a tourist.

_____

_____

3. My father almost earned three thousand dollars more for the additional work.

_____

_____

4. She read the story about Little Ann with her sister.

_____

_____

5. He caught sight of a spider talking to his mother.

_____

_____

Bears

How many types of bears do you know? Some well recognized types are the polar bear, black bear, brown bear, and honey bear.

Polar bears live in the Arctic. They eat marine animals and birds. Polar bears are covered in thick white fur so that they can hide in the snow. They also have a layer of insulating fat to help them survive the extreme cold. Not only are polar bears the greatest hunters of all the bears, they can also swim 100 kilometres without stopping to rest!

The black bear weighs about 136 kilograms, which is about as heavy as two adults. It averages 1.8 metres long, the height of a tall man. Like all bears that live in cold climates, the black bear hibernates throughout winter.

Brown bears can be found in Europe, Asia, and North America. One of the best known types of brown bears is the grizzly bear, which can weigh as much as 450 kg! Grizzlies also hibernate throughout winter.

The largest of all the bears is a type of brown bear called the Kodiak bear. At 2.75 m tall, it weighs as much as 725 kg – almost as much as eight people combined. Kodiaks eat plants and roots, but they really love fish, especially salmon. Every year, large groups of Kodiaks gather in streams to catch salmon as they swim their way upstream to the spawning grounds.

Honey bears live in Southeast Asia and are only 1.2 m long and weigh 45 kg, making them the smallest of all bear species.

The headline in the *Toronto Star* on August 27, 2005 was bad news for bears. It read, "Fish Bad for Grizzlies". If bears eat fish rather than berries and plants, they would have a high level of pollutants in their bodies, because the fish are swimming in polluted waters. When they get contaminated, they pass the pollutants on to the bears.

Maybe one day you will have a job as a naturalist. It might be your responsibility to track and count bear populations, record the changes to their habitats, and suggest ways of protecting them.

A. **Complete the following chart with information from the passage.**

BEARS

Name	Physical Appearance	Characteristics
Polar		
Black		
Grizzly		
Kodiak		
Honey		

B. **Answer the following questions.**

1. Which type of bear impresses you the most? Why?

_____

2. Grizzlies enjoy eating fish but why are fish bad for them?

_____

3. Why do you think naturalists have to track and count bear populations and record the changes to their habitats?

_____

_____

_____

_____

Did You Know?

The teddy bear was named after U.S. President Theodore "Teddy" Roosevelt who, in 1902, set free a helpless bear during a hunting trophy.

Date : _____

Writing Interesting Sentences

Inverting Word Order

Inverting the order of the words in a sentence can give it a fresh look and make it more interesting.

Example: The geese flew in unison across the blue sky.
Across the blue sky the geese flew in unison.
Or: In unison across the blue sky flew the geese.

A. Invert the word order in the following sentences to make them sound more interesting.

1. A crimson sun set over the plain.

    _____

2. The players assembled in the locker room for a pep talk.

    _____

3. What she wanted to eat was fish and chips.

    _____

4. He moved deftly to the side to avoid the tag.

    _____

5. The firefighters raced against time to save her from the flood.

    _____

6. The motorbike sped through the narrow alley.

    _____

7. He scored the winning run with two out and one on third base.

    _____

    _____

8. The kites flew gracefully in the breeze.

    _____

    _____

Adding Details

Adding details and descriptive language is another way of making sentences interesting.

Examples: We played on the beach.
We built sandcastles on the quiet, beautiful beach.
They had a game of baseball.
They played an exciting game of baseball after school.

B. Add details to the following sentences. Use additional phrases and clauses where necessary.

1. They went on a trip.

    _____

2. The snow began to fall.

    _____

3. We watched the show.

    _____

4. Fall is a beautiful season.

    _____

5. The bus was full.

    _____

6. The boat sailed on the waterway.

    _____

C. Expand what Michael says in three different ways.

The ride is exciting!

1. _____

    _____

2. _____

3. _____

Hidden Depths

Three quarters of the Earth's surface is covered in water. Until recently, we did not have the technology to go deep enough or to shed enough light on the ocean floor to see what was swimming about in that vast undersea world. But now, oceanographers are doing just that.

Oceanographers are scientists who study the ocean and its life forms. In 2005, 24 scientists from the United States, Canada, Russia, and China went on a joint underwater venture in the Canadian Basin in the Arctic Ocean. They were on the American Coast Guard cutter Healy. These scientists were collecting species never known before! The mission's Chief Scientist Dr. Ronald Keith O'Dor, a professor of marine biology at Dalhousie University in Halifax, called the project "wet NASA". Like NASA's exploration of space, they were going into the vast unknown areas of the ocean that can only be accessed by specialized vehicles and life support systems.

It was O'Dor's dream to see a Giant Squid in that unknown part of the world. For over 2000 years, this behemoth creature has evoked both fear and fascination. Although O'Dor himself did not see the Giant Squid in his exploration, some Japanese scientists captured the creature on film later that year. They believe it was the first time that the Giant Squid was photographed in its natural habitat. All the Giant Squids that had ever been found before were dead and washed ashore. These photographs were a major leap for the scientific community, and would open the door to more detailed studies.

O'Dor must have been very pleased to hear this good news.

A. Give one-word answers from the passage to the following questions.

1. What is the study of living things? _____

2. What is a two-syllable adjective to do with water? _____

3. What is a word that rhymes with "imagination"? _____

4. What is the acronym for the National Aeronautics and Space Administration? _____

5. Who are the people that study the ocean and its life forms? _____

6. Name the capital city of Nova Scotia. _____

7. Find a word contained in "adventure". _____

8. What is another word for "something huge"? _____

B. Answer the following questions.

1. What were the countries involved in the "wet NASA" project?

_____

2. Why did Professor Ronald O'Dor call the project "wet NASA"?

_____

_____

3. How do scientists access unknown areas of the ocean?

_____

4. How do you think the photographs of the Giant Squid will be useful?

_____

_____

_____

_____

_____

Did You Know?

The Giant Squid is the world's largest invertebrate. It can be up to 18 metres long and weigh up to 900 kilograms. Scientists suspect it lives mostly at depths of 200 to 800 metres.

Day
66

Concise Writing

Clear and concise writing makes it easy for the reader to understand the ideas we want to convey. Remember these points when writing sentences and paragraphs:

– Separate sentences that contain more than one idea into two.
– Combine short sentences that contain related ideas into one sentence.
– Simplify overloaded sentences by cutting out unnecessary details or descriptions.
– The main idea in all the sentences in a paragraph should be related.

A.   **Improve the group of sentences below using the above guidance.**

1.   The weather report called for sunny sky and mild temperature and Jason thought it was a good idea to go on a bike ride so he invited his friend Ron to join him on a bike ride.

_____

_____

_____

2.   Ron rode a 12-speed bike. He received the bike for his birthday last year. It was from his grandfather. Jason's was a 10-speed bike. It was given to him by his brother. The bike was like new.

_____

_____

3.   The two rode for an hour. They stopped for refreshment and some rest. Part of the ride was up a long slope and they were very tired. They were not used to riding uphill.

_____

_____

B. **Put each group of related ideas below in one sentence.**

Decide on the order of presenting
the ideas before writing.

Example: *Rita wanted to buy a bicycle.*
She wanted to buy an 18-speed mountain bike.
She decided to save her allowance.

Because Rita wanted to buy an 18-speed mountain bike, she
decided to save her allowance.

1. Many flights were delayed or cancelled.

   There was a severe snowstorm.

   The airport was crowded.

   The passengers were waiting anxiously in the airport.

   _____

   _____

2. Paul was a responsible boy.

   He delivered newspapers.

   He delivered newspapers seven days a week.

   He delivered newspapers even in bad weather.

   _____

   _____

3. The cave was pitch dark.

   The cave was eerie.

   The children held their breath.

   They dared not make a sound.

   _____

   _____

Bear Attack

More and more people like backpacking and hiking. Is there anything that one cannot appreciate about the rugged mountainous terrain, fresh air, and the majestic beauty of the wilderness? Yet a lot of us forget that many of the original inhabitants of these areas still live there, including bears.

In the back country, we are in fact the intruders, though most of our intrusions will go unnoticed by the natural inhabitants. Bears, for example, are more curious than aggressive. They may approach, but will usually run if they sense that you are aware of their presence. It is not unusual to see bears on the trail in daylight hours although most of the sightings will be in the evening.

Should you be confronted by a bear on the rare occasion, there are ways to protect yourself. If it is going to attack, keep a cool head. The worst thing you can do is panic and run. Never try to outrun a bear because it moves much faster than you think. An average bear can run up to 40 kilometres an hour!

Also, never remove your backpack. Some people feel that the extra weight will hamper their agility in a confrontation with a bear. In fact, your backpack provides extra protection for your body if the bear grabs or rolls on you.

If the bear looks like it is going into a full confrontation, drop to the ground, roll into a fetal position, and cover your head, chest, and abdomen by rolling yourself into a tight ball. These are the crucial areas to be protected. Usually, if you allow the bear to roll on you while you are still in a tight ball, the bear will give up and deem you dead. It will wander away.

Eliciting Information

When we need to elicit information about something, there are six important questions to keep in mind. As Benjamin Franklin wrote, "I kept six honest serving men, they taught me all I know. Their names were Who and What and When and Why and Where and How."

A. **Form questions to elicit information about the passage using Franklin's six honest serving men.**

Five "W"s and "How"

1. Who

   _____

2. What

   _____

3. When

   _____

4. Why

   _____

5. Where

   _____

6. How

   _____

B. **Design a notice to advise hikers how to react in the event of a bear attack.**

Day **68**

Date : _____

Similes and Metaphors

Similes

A **simile** is a comparison of two things that have some characteristics in common.

Examples: He runs as fast as a deer.
                     She sang like a nightingale.

The two things that are being compared are linked by "as" or "like".

A. **Enrich each of the following sentences with a simile. Use "as" or "like".**

Example: He was very brave.
                    He was as brave as a lion.

1. The sports car sped past me.

    _____

2. The children were very happy.

    _____

3. The plane soared.

    _____

4. Her mother was very angry.

    _____

5. The room was dark.

    _____

6. The boy is chubby.

    _____

7. The shoes were shiny.

    _____

Metaphors

A **metaphor** is another form of comparison without using "as" or "like". In using a metaphor, we are describing something as though it were something else.

Example: He has a heart of stone.   (metaphor)
He has a heart like a stone.   (simile)

B.   Underline the metaphorical terms.

1.   The highway is the artery of the province.

2.   The troubled teenager is a bear to deal with.

3.   Friendship is the sunshine in life.

4.   To Matt, home is a prison.

5.   He examined the diamond with a vulture's eye.

C.   Try using similes or metaphors to enliven the following sentences. You may change some words in the sentences if necessary.

1.   The dark clouds hung low in the sky.

_____

2.   He swam swiftly to the raft.

_____

3.   The batter was keyed up waiting for the next pitch.

_____

4.   After the trip, he was exhausted.

_____

5.   She is kind to everyone.

_____

6.   The afternoon sun is hot.

_____

Advice Column

Advice columns are a great way for people to get help with their problems. They are commonly found in magazines and newspapers. Here is an example of what a child might write to an advice column called "Helpful Harry".

Dear Helpful Harry,

I told my best friend a really important secret, and he promised that he wouldn't tell anyone. At first I really trusted him. After all, he is my best friend. A couple of days later everyone at school knew what my secret was. He says he didn't tell anyone, but I don't know if I believe him. How else could have everyone found out what my secret was? Do you think I should still be his friend, even though he's telling everyone all of my secrets?

Sincerely,

Disappointed

Dear Disappointed,

If your friend says that he didn't tell anyone, what makes you so sure that he really did? Has he ever done anything like this before? Is it at all possible that the other students in your school found out what your secret was in another way? After all, you did say that he is your best friend. Ask your friend, and let him know how hurt you are that people know your secret. If he says that he didn't tell anyone, maybe you should accept that. The next time you tell him a secret, if everyone else seems to find out, then you should consider whether or not he's really that good a friend, but for now, don't ruin a good friendship.

Sincerely,

Helpful Harry

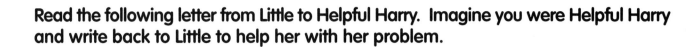

Read the following letter from Little to Helpful Harry. Imagine you were Helpful Harry and write back to Little to help her with her problem.

Saturday, March 4, 2006

_____

_____

_____

_____

_____

_____

_____

_____

_____

_____

_____

Dear Helpful Harry,

I'm really short and I have trouble reaching things that are high up. As if that wasn't bad enough, everyone at school is always teasing me. It's really not fair to make fun of me just because I'm shorter than they are. My mom and dad say that I'll grow taller later, but I want to be taller now. I'm tired of always being picked on.

How can I make people stop teasing me?

Sincerely,

Little

Did You Know?

Many advice columnists use pen names instead of their real names. For example, the original "Ann Landers" – the famous column that ran in newspapers throughout North America for almost 50 years – was a nurse named Ruth Crowley. After she died, a woman named Esther Pauline Lederer took over.

YOU Deserve A Break!

Read the clues and complete the crossword puzzle on sports.

Across

A. You need to run a long distance in this sport.

B. You need a board with four wheels to play this sport.

C. You play this sport on a diamond.

D. You shoot with a bow and arrows.

E. You need a boat and a double-bladed paddle to play this sport.

F. You glide on snow using a pair of long, flat runners.

Down

1. You score points by throwing a ball through a hoop.

2. Only the goalie can touch the ball with the hands in this sport.

3. You need a shuttlecock to play this sport.

4. You sail while standing on a sailboard.

5. You play this sport on ice with a curved stick.

6. You propel a small, hard ball with various clubs into a hole.

Add Colour to Your Writing

Descriptive Language

You can enhance your writing by using vivid language to replace ordinary, less colourful words.

Example: The word "big" might be replaced by "huge", "gigantic", or "enormous".

A. **For each sentence, replace the underlined word with a more descriptive word from the list of words provided.**

scampered   ecstatic   cavernous   considerate   towering

1. The big (   ) canyon could not be crossed.

2. As soon as the rain stopped, the children ran (   ) out to play.

3. Everyone likes him because he is nice (   ).

4. The players were happy (   ) to have won three times in a row.

5. The tall (   ) cliff appears to be rising straight out of the sea.

B. **Complete the following passage with the descriptive words on the left.**

cool
green
refresh
leaning
peaceful
swooped
towering
swaying
gentle
enjoy

The 1._____ river flowed calmly through the

2._____ valley. On both sides of the river grew

3._____ oaks with branches 4._____

and 5._____ towards the riverbank. Birds

6._____ down to 7._____ a drink of

8._____ water. Forest animals also came to the

bank to 9._____ themselves. Life in the valley

was 10._____ .

Padded language occurs when we become wordy. Sometimes it is the use of clauses or phrases where a single word would suffice. Generally, clear, concise sentences are more effective and easy to read.

Example: What he wants to do is to become a professional basketball player. (wordy)

He wants to become a professional basketball player. (concise)

C. **Rewrite the following sentences in a more concise way.**

1. The reason we want to go to the park is that we want to have a game of baseball.

   _____

2. In my opinion, I don't think it is proper to do that.

   _____

3. According to what I remember, they broke the record two years ago.

   _____

4. The fact is that she doesn't seem to realize the crux of the problem.

   _____

5. In actual fact, they were all eager to take part in it.

   _____

6. Due to the fact that today is a public holiday, the malls are closed.

   _____

7. He saw the key which was in the lock.

   _____

8. It occurs to me that I may be late if I don't hurry.

   _____

Sweden's Road Charge

Think of the air above the planet as the greenhouse that surrounds our world. Picture it as a protective bubble that stops the sun from burning up our habitat. Nations around the world have agreed that this thin layer of air which protects our planet and allows life to exist must be protected – it is our "greenhouse". That is why many of them have signed an agreement called the Kyoto Accord. It is an agreement for every country to reduce its greenhouse gas emissions.

Although nearly every country has agreed to reduce toxic emissions, such as exhaust from cars and factories, few have actually done anything to deal with the problem. Sweden is one of the few countries that have. In fact, Sweden is one of the leaders in adhering to Kyoto's clean air program. Even so, each year more and more people move into Stockholm, the country's capital city, adding to traffic pollution. Already, Stockholm has traffic assistance teams who sit for 24 hours a day in front of rows of TV screens that monitor all of the major commuter highways. These teams can redirect traffic, post messages on programmable signs, shut down lanes, or even close entire tunnel ways.

Since January of 2006, engineers have been trying another means of reducing traffic congestion. At least temporarily, Stockholm is charging visitors to the city a border crossing fee. The plan is to reduce rush hour congestion by 10% to 15%. Drivers are required to pay higher rates during the morning and afternoon rush hours. The idea is that these fees will encourage car pooling and reduce the number of cars on the road, which in turn reduce emissions. The fees are lower during the middle of the workday when there is not as much traffic. Taxis and environmental vehicles, including hybrid cars and Sweden's own bio-gas fuelled cars, are given exemptions to this charge.

The income from this program will be spent on improving public transit. Despite Stockholm's already world-class rail and bus options, an improved transit system will encourage people to leave their cars at home. The program will be undergoing an 18-month trial, after which residents of the city can vote on whether or not to keep it.

A. Write the main idea of each paragraph in one or two sentences.

Paragraph 1 _____
_____
_____

Paragraph 2 _____
_____
_____

Paragraph 3 _____
_____
_____

Paragraph 4 _____
_____
_____

B. Do you think the model in Sweden can be adopted in Canadian cities? Why or why not? What else can we do to reduce greenhouse gas emissions? Write your own response.

_____
_____
_____
_____
_____
_____

Imagery in Poetry

When we write a poem, we are creating images that make readers use their imagination. There are several ways to do so:

1. Using similes: comparing two things using "like" or "as"
    Example: He is as agile as a leopard.

2. Using metaphors: comparing two unlike things
    Example: Life is a sandglass.

3. Using personification: giving human qualities to inanimate things
    Example: The sun smiled upon the flowers.

A. Complete each description below with a simile.

1. a smile like _____

2. as cunning as _____

3. as strong as _____

4. with leaves like _____

5. as smooth as _____

6. as dazzling as _____

7. with legs like _____

8. dark as _____

B. Rewrite the following sentences using metaphors.

1. The sun shone brightly over the lake.

    _____

2. The heavy rain fell on the parched land.

    _____

3. His smile warms everyone's heart.

    _____

4. The wounded soldier dropped on the ground.

    _____

5. Time waits for no one.

    _____

C. Complete the following sentences with verbs that personify the inanimate subjects.

1. The snowflakes _____ in the air.

2. The wind _____ the flowers.

3. The weeping willow _____ along the river.

4. The renovated house _____ its occupants.

5. The sea _____ up to the shore.

6. The stone _____ the tranquil lake.

7. The morning sun _____ the campers.

D. Complete the verse with figurative language. You may use similes, metaphors, or personification.

A Stormy Night

Dark clouds _____

Raindrops _____

Lightning _____

Thunder _____

Bio-gas Fuelled Cars

Cars use gasoline for fuel, but are there really no other options? Of course there are! Options include electric hybrids and bio-gas fuelled cars. It's a wonder we still use gasoline at all.

Sweden, a country that has always been among the leaders of clean air and pollution reducing techniques, has been using one of these other options for quite some time. Bio-fuel powered Volvo vehicles can be found all over the country. The vehicles run on methane, which is a bio-gas. Methane is produced when living things decay. Sewers and water treatment plants produce methane. When we "pass gas", we are also letting out a form of methane.

Methane-fuelled cars are highly efficient. Carbon dioxide emissions from a bio-gas fuelled car are about 25% lower than those from a petrol engine. A car running on methane contributes almost nothing to the global warming problem caused by greenhouse gases.

Sweden currently has 21 plants producing bio-gas for vehicles. Of these, nine use raw sewage sludge. Other plants use anything from household scraps to slaughterhouse waste and even food industry leftovers.

As pollution increases and gasoline prices continue to soar, bio-gas could be a very real solution to our current fuel problems. There are 69 filling stations in Sweden and plans for another 40 by 2006. Sweden has over 5300 bio-gas fuelled vehicles already. Although most of them are cars, there are some other heavy vehicles and buses that have made the switch to bio-gas as well.

By 2020, there could be over one million cars running on this alternative fuel system. With Sweden leading the way to a new alternative fuel, we can only wonder why other countries continue to drag their heels.

A. Answer the following questions.

1. Why do we have to consider other fuel options?

   _____

2. How is methane produced in Sweden?

   _____

   _____

3. Which sentence shows that many countries are reluctant to consider switching to using bio-gas?

   _____

4. Which sentence indicates that bio-gas fuelled cars will become more and more popular?

   _____

   _____

B. Imagine you were a bio-gas fuelled car salesperson. Explain to your potential customer why they should consider buying a bio-gas fuelled car instead of a gas car.

   _____

   _____

   _____

   _____

   _____

   _____

   _____

Did You Know?

The world's first passenger train that runs on bio-gas had its first journey in Sweden in the fall of 2005.

Acrostic Poems

An **acrostic poem** is a poem in which the first letters of the lines form a word or words.

Example: ADAM SMITH

Always smart and bright   **S**ailing in summer we go
Doing everything right   **M**aking kites to fly together
Adam is my best friend   **I**n beautiful fall weather
Many happy times we spend   **T**oday is Adam's birthday
                                    Happy may he forever stay

Although the lines in an acrostic poem don't have to rhyme, it's always more fun to read lines that do.

A. **As warm-up, write three rhyming words for each of the following lead words.**

1. celebrate

2. fine

3. jog

4. snow

5. freezing

6. summer

7. peace

8. pouring

9. shimmer

10. foggy

11. night

B. Write an acrostic poem with your first name. Make the lines rhyme where possible.

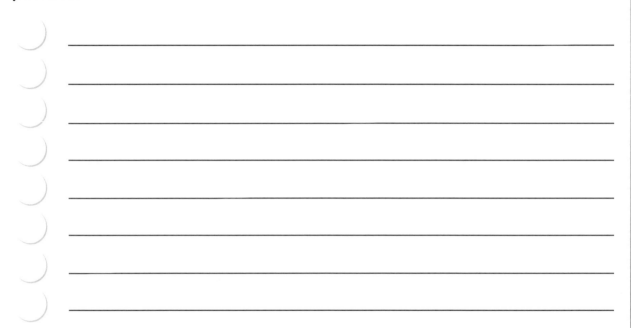

_____

_____

_____

_____

_____

_____

_____

C. Try writing another acrostic poem, this time with your best friend's first name.

_____

_____

_____

_____

_____

_____

_____

_____

Do Cell Phones Cause Accidents?

More and more people are using cell phones while they drive. You've seen them. Your parents may have the same habit as well. According to the National Highway Traffic Safety Administration in the United States, there has been a 50% increase in cell phone use while driving since 2002.

With so many people talking and driving, accidents occur. If people had been using their cell phone just before an accident, would they admit they were distracted by the conversation on the cell phone? Of course not! Many states are attempting to put a stop to it and have already banned the use of hand-held cell phones in the car.

The Insurance Institute for Highway Safety recently did a study that compared cell phone use during accidents by examining cell phone records. The study shows drivers regardless of age or sex that use their cell phone while driving are four times more likely to be in an accident that results in injury. The study examined 456 drivers in Perth, Australia who owned or used mobile phones and were in a crash that required a hospital emergency room visit between April 2002 and July 2004.

Nine out of 10 people who had used their cell phone just before an accident suffered at least one injury, while nearly half had two or more. Most of the injuries were not severe. Nearly 75% of the accidents occurred in clear weather conditions. Over 90% of the accidents involved other vehicles, and nearly 50% of the injured drivers said that the accident occurred within 10 minutes of the start of their trip.

What do you think? Are people who use their cell phone more likely to be involved in an accident? Are they more distracted because of talking on the phone? Should hand-held cell phones be banned?

When you take sides on an issue, you need to defend your viewpoint. The following exercise will enable you to practise doing that.

A. Pretend you were a safety expert advising an insurance company on whether or not hand-held cell phones should be banned while driving.

1. Write three points you will use in favour of the ban.

_____

_____

_____

2. Write a conclusion sentence in favour of the ban.

_____

_____

B. Now pretend you were an executive for a cell phone company. Present an argument against banning cell phones while driving.

1. Write three points you will use against the ban.

_____

_____

_____

2. Write a conclusion sentence opposing the ban.

_____

_____

_____

_____

Did You Know?

The reason why it is dangerous to talk on the phone while driving is that our brain cannot give full attention to what we see and what we hear at the same time. Driving is mostly a visual task, while talking on the phone requires a lot of listening.

Troubleshooting Confusing Writing

Possessive Adjectives

Sometimes it is the use of pronouns or possessive adjectives that leads to confusion.

Example: When Kate saw Joanne, she greeted her.
(We do not know who greeted whom.)
When Kate saw Joanne, Kate greeted her.

A. Rewrite the following sentences to remove the confusion.

1. Andrew asked Peter to explain his problem.

    _____

2. Janice told her best friend Mandy that she had won the first prize.

    _____

3. The girls in grade six competed against the boys and they lost.

    _____

4. Rob met Sam when he first joined the school team.

    _____

5. Matt argued with Paul and he was furious.

    _____

6. The father and the son did not know what to do so he suggested putting it aside first.

    _____

    _____

7. The Jays and the Yankees each scored a run in the seventh inning, and they were confident that they would tie the game soon.

    _____

    _____

Word Order

Sometimes it is the word order that confuses the reader.

Example: Being the youngest child in the family, everyone takes good care of Jim.

(It appears as if "everyone" is the youngest child in the family, not Jim.)

Jim being the youngest child in the family, everyone takes good care of him.

Or: Being the youngest child in the family, Jim is taken good care of by everyone.

B.   Change the word order in the following sentences to correct the confusion.

1.   He saw Ashley's dog walking to school.

_____

_____

2.   She almost spent all of her savings. Now she is poor.

_____

3.   He told his family about his brush with death after he was rescued.

_____

4.   Being the youngest in the family, no one listens to Mike.

_____

5.   Laughing out loud, the naughty monkey entertained the children.

_____

6.   He talked endlessly about his exciting trip last Sunday.

_____

7.   The children spotted a big fish sailing down the river.

_____

Timepieces

Imagine a watch that not only tells time and functions as an alarm clock, but even allows you to access up-to-the-minute information like news, weather, sports scores, and movie times.

A "smart watch" is one such device. Smart watches are new, high-tech watches that have in them Microsoft's SPOT, or Smart Personal Objects Technology.

These watches can be synchronized with the calendar program on your computer. That way, you can have reminders and appointments from your calendar while you're on the move. Your parents and friends can even send you messages with MSN Messenger.

The best part is that all this information is transmitted wirelessly, and is available in 12 of Canada's largest cities as well as 100 cities in the United States. Called MSNDirect, the service is delivered through FM radio waves. What's more, if you travel to a different city, the watch automatically updates itself with the time, weather, and news from wherever you are, so your watch is always up to date.

The clock was a great invention and as people came to rely more and more on it, there was soon a need for it to be more portable. Since the creation of the first watch, designers have continually sought to improve it. From the traditional pocket watch to the more portable wrist-watch, to the dawn of the digital watch, designers have continuously been seeking ways to improve this incredible device. Watches soon included alarms in addition to being able to keep time. As they became more and more advanced, more and more gadgets were added to them, including compasses and calendars.

Now that the Internet has also become essential to our culture, it isn't at all surprising that we are combining it with the watch.

A. **Use the passage and the Internet to find out what each of these stands for.**

1. **SPOT** _____

2. **MSN** _____

3. **FM** _____

B. **Answer the following questions.**

1. List two advantages of the smart watch.

_____

_____

2. How widely available is the MSNDirect service?

_____

_____

3. Besides a calendar, what other gadget can be added to a watch?

_____

4. Do you foresee any other smart devices? If so, what are they? If not, why?

_____

_____

5. Are smart devices a sign of technological progress? Why or why not?

_____

_____

6. Are smart devices a sign of cultural progress? Why or why not?

_____

_____

Date : _____

Writing Paragraphs

A **paragraph** is made up of a group of sentences with a common topic. The first sentence of a paragraph is usually the **topic sentence**. It states the main idea of the paragraph. The sentences that follow the topic sentence explain the main idea further or add details to it.

A. **In each group of sentences below, use numbers to indicate how the sentences should be arranged to make a coherent paragraph. Use "1" for the topic sentence.**

1.

_____ In fact, it is the third largest live theatre centre in the world.

_____ It has a population of more than 3 000 000.

_____ There are many theatres in Toronto.

_____ Toronto is the biggest city in Canada.

2.

_____ Matt always enjoys his time there.

_____ They have a boat for water-skiing too.

_____ Every summer, Matt and his family spend a month in their cottage on Georgian Bay.

_____ In their cottage, there is a dock for swimming.

3.

_____ Without his sacrifice fly, we wouldn't have won yesterday's game against the Warriors.

_____ Jeff is the best hitter on our team.

_____ He has scored more runs than any of us this season.

_____ Jeff is also a team-player; he doesn't just think about himself.

B. **Write a topic sentence for each of the following paragraphs. Your topic sentence should introduce the main idea of the sentences in the paragraph.**

1. Topic sentence: _____

   _____

   We use the computer to research and do projects. We keep in touch with our friends by e-mail or instant messaging. For entertainment we play online games. Our parents manage their finance and do their banking on computer too. It's hard to think back to the days when there was no computer.

2. Topic sentence: _____

   _____

   It is estimated that more than a billion people use English today. Half of these use English as their second language. English is now the language of business with over 80% of the world's telecommunications, faxes, and e-mails in English. The desire for the world's population to learn English has spawned numerous educational agencies that arrange for English language classes in many Asian countries.

3. Topic sentence: _____

   _____

   Gretzky was not big in stature, nor was he particularly fast on skates. However, he had the ability to control the offence of the game. He established an all-time scoring record with 215 total points in a single season. When Gretzky retired in 1999, fans were saddened at the prospect that such a great player would never play again.

You Deserve A Break!

Unscramble the words and write them on the correct boards in alphabetical order. Colour the insects on the brick wall.

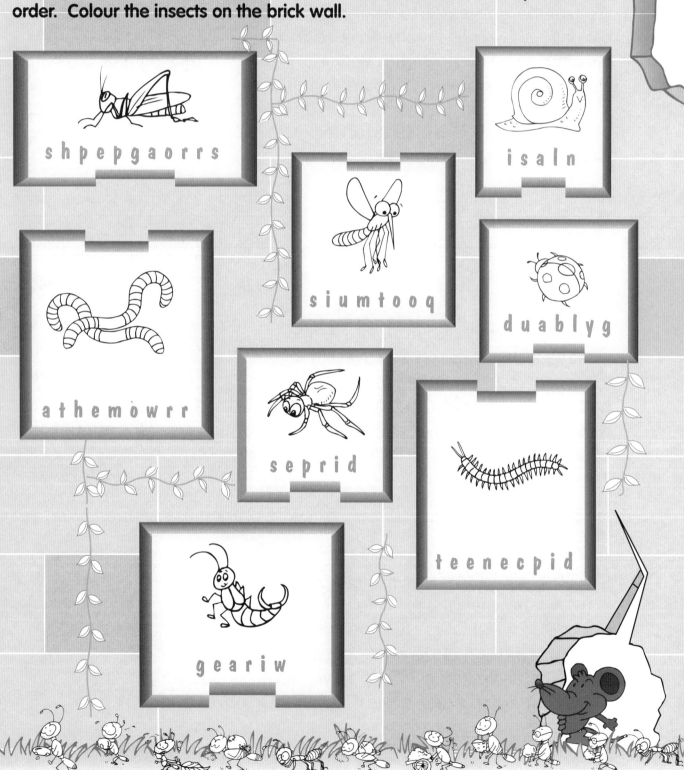

shpepgaorrs

isaln

siumtooq

duablyg

athemowrr

seprid

teenecpid

geariw

Insect

Non-insect

Holograms

If you wanted to take a picture of your room, you might take a picture of one wall and then another, and then the other two, then the floor, and finally the ceiling. Now you have photographs of the entire room, but they aren't connected like your room is; each one is separate and putting them together isn't quite the same. It just looks like a line of two-dimensional pictures.

A hologram, by contrast, is a three-dimensional "recording" of something. A hologram of your room would therefore resemble a cube instead of a flat line of pictures. Maybe you've seen a baseball or magic card where the picture is so lifelike that it seems to pop out at you. That is a hologram.

Look! The ball seems to be flying out of the card!

To make a hologram, you need two beams of light: one to illuminate the object to be recorded, and one to hit a glass photographic plate – the "film" – where the hologram is recorded. The two beams actually come from one single laser beam. What happens is that the laser beam is fired at a mirror, which splits it in two. One beam goes off in one direction to light up the object while the other hits another mirror. Then each of the two beams bounces back to meet at the photographic plate – placed between the object and the second mirror – to form a pattern. This pattern is the three-dimensional "recording" of the object.

Gabor discovered the hologram and received the Nobel Prize in Physics for it in 1971. It was refined and developed further by other physicists, who are scientists that study the physical properties of matter and motion.

The most common type of hologram is the rainbow hologram. It can be mass copied and viewed with regular, or white, light. Rainbow holograms have appeared on magazine covers and are used on credit cards so people cannot counterfeit them.

Visual Representations

Visual representations, such as diagrams, are especially helpful when you need to understand a piece of writing with technical or scientific concepts. The passage you have just read deals with a topic in physics, and may require some rereading. This is when making a visual representation of the text will help you.

A. Complete the following diagram by adding missing labels and tracing the beams of light.

photographic plate

object to be recorded

mirror one

mirror two

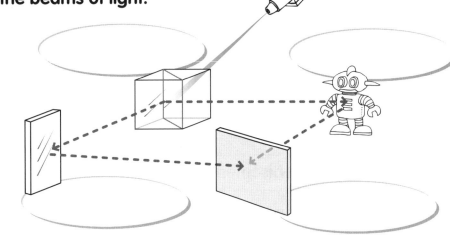

B. Fill in the blanks with words from the passage.

1. In order to take a picture of something, you need to _____ it with a light source.

2. If pictures speak a thousand words, do you think these _____ can serve as visual essays?

3. Physics, chemistry, and biology are all fields of study where theories and experiments need to be continuously _____ .

4. Some people have very elaborate signatures so that nobody can _____ them.

5. A single _____ can be as sharp as a knife.

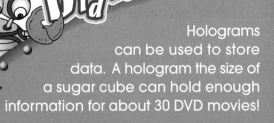

Writing Ads

Newspaper advertisements are often kept short to save space and cost. They contain only the crucial information, leaving out the detailed descriptions.

Example: A "For Rent" ad

This cottage is located on a quiet lake just three hours north of the city. It is spacious and can accommodate up to eight people. It is also ideal for children because there is a safe sandy beach close to it. Included in the rental is a motor boat, which is ideal for water activities. The weekly rate is $1000.

are best offer.

Cottage for Rent

Lakefront cottage. Sleeps eight. Boat, beach, safe swimming. Ideal for children. 3 hours from city. $1000/week.

Garage Sale

A. Write a brief advertisement for each of the following.

1. **Want Ad – Delivery Boy/Girl**

   We are a busy grocery looking for a reliable, responsible youth to take up delivery responsibilities in the neighbourhood after school and on weekends. He or she must be friendly and enjoys meeting people. A bicycle will be provided. We offer an hourly rate of $8.00.

   Ad

   _____

   _____

   _____

   _____

   _____

2. **House for Rent**

   This house is a back-split bungalow located within walking distance from a shopping mall and transportation. There is a garage for two cars and a huge backyard. The kitchen has just been renovated. The basement is finished with an entertainment room and a washroom. It is an ideal family home. The rental rate is $1500 a month.

   Ad

   _____

   _____

   _____

   _____

   _____

3. **Bike for Sale**

This is an 18-speed, 42-cm-frame mountain bike, black with red racing stripes. It is like new, with excellent gears and a comfortable gel-padded seat. It comes with reflectors, a kickstand, and a carrier. It is offered for sale for $120. This is a bargain because the bike has only been used for a few times.

Ad

_____

_____

_____

_____

_____

B. **Read the ad and write a more detailed description of the garage sale based on it.**

here,
unday
niture
real
ronics
orts &

Garage Sale

18 Woody Dr. July 6, 10 – 4.
Furniture, clothing, toys,
books, sports equipment,
etc. Everything must go.

Garage Sale

Gara
Octo
Appl
other
sofas
are f

_____

_____

_____

_____

_____

_____

_____

_____

_____

Facts about Hurricanes

Hurricanes are severe tropical storms with winds of 64 knots – 118 kilometres per hour – or more. The winds of a hurricane spiral inward toward the storm centre, creating the "eye" which is easy to distinguish on an aerial tracking satellite. Since the 1950s, each hurricane has been tracked, rated, and named to characterize its destructive potential. In addition to wind speed and pressure, other factors to consider when classifying hurricanes are the height of the water that surges onto the coast, and the potential destruction that results.

There are five levels of classification for hurricanes, with "five" being the most severe – the rarest of them all. Before Katrina, Hurricane Andrew in 1992 was the last catastrophic storm to go through the United States. Shrubs and trees were blown down, and the roofs of most buildings were damaged. The glass in windows shattered, and doors were blown out of buildings. Small buildings were blown away altogether, and mobile homes were completely destroyed. The lower floors of all structures less than eight metres above sea level near the shore were extensively damaged. Inland escape routes were cut off by rising water three to five hours before the storm even arrived. Massive evacuation was ordered.

Hurricane Charley in 2004 was in category four; it was an "extreme" hurricane. The same damage caused by Andrew occurred to roofs, doors, windows, mobile homes, shrubs, and trees. The difference was that the flooding did not penetrate as far inland, nor did the flood waters rise as high. Massive evacuation was ordered but not of as wide an area.

On average, there are about 10 named tropical storms off the east coast of the United States each year, but only two to three are likely to reach category three or greater intensity.

Since 1979, men's and women's names have been alternated for naming hurricanes, and the names are on a rotation to appear again after several years. Names make the storms easier to track and record damage. The only time a name may not be used again is if a storm is so deadly or costly that the future use of its name on a different storm would cause people pain in remembering. Andrew has been struck off the list, and most likely Katrina will be, too.

Read the chart below to answer the questions in point form.

Hurricane Categories

Category	Damage	Wind (kph)	Water Surge (m)
1	minimal	74 – 95	1 – 1.5
2	moderate	96 – 110	2 – 2.5
3	extensive	111 – 130	3 – 3.5
4	extreme	131 – 155	4 – 5.5
5	catastrophic	>155	>5.5

1. What would have been the wind speed and water surge of Hurricane Andrew?

   _____

2. What are the wind speed and water surge of a hurricane that causes minimal damage?

   _____

3. If a hurricane has a wind speed of 125 kilometres per hour and builds a water surge of three metres, what category is it and what will be the level of damage?

   _____

Challenge

Do you think using men's and women's names is the best way to name hurricanes? Why or why not? Can you think of other ways of naming hurricanes? Describe your method and explain why it might be better.

_____

_____

_____

_____

Day **84**

The Factual Composition (1)

Organizing Facts

Before we write a **factual composition**, it is important that we group the facts and organize them into a logical sequence for presentation.

Steps:

1. List the facts you want to include in your writing.
2. Group them according to a common topic.
3. Decide on the order of presentation in your writing, i.e. which group of facts should come first, which should come next, and so on.

Read the list of facts about the Giant Squid. Group the related facts and write the numbers under the respective headings.

The Giant Squid's physical appearance

_____

Living habits

_____

What we don't know about the Giant Squid

_____

Facts about the Giant Squid

1. Sperm whales like eating Giant Squids.

2. Scientists estimate that the Giant Squid can grow to be 25 metres long.

3. They live at depths between 200 and 800 metres.

4. They can change their colour and shape to blend in with their environment.

5. What they eat still remains a mystery.

6. They can weigh as much as 500 kilograms.

7. They have eyes larger than the headlights of a car.

8. They have eight muscular arms that can reach a length of 3 metres.

9. Their mouth is at the centre of the arms.

10. They obtain oxygen through a pair of long gills.

11. We do not know if Giant Squids live alone or in groups.

12. They have a large, elongated sac that is full of black, mucous ink that is used as an escape method to confuse predators.

13. They swim fast to escape from their predators.

14. They can be twice as long as a school bus.

15. The largest Giant Squid was found on a beach in New Zealand in 1880. It measured about 20 metres in length.

16. Scientists still do not know the precise habitat of the Giant Squid.

17. Neither do scientists know how long they can actually grow.

18. The Giant Squid has the largest eyes of any animal in the animal kingdom.

19. We do not know how they distribute in the oceans.

The Destruction of New Orleans

In the wake of Hurricane Katrina, people were trapped inside flooded houses, stranded on rooftops, and huddled on overpasses leading out of the flooded city. New Orleans Mayor Ray Nagin had called repeatedly for aid from the Federal Government, but without prompt response. To make the problem worse, many people remained behind despite warnings to evacuate. After all, the city had survived hurricane Camille in 1969, and thus many people believed that Katrina would not do enough damage to justify their evacuating the city. Unfortunately, they were wrong.

The destruction left by Katrina was insurmountable. But the damage was not caused by the winds alone. Although the hurricane itself did incredible damage, the flooding that followed was even worse. Flood waters covered 80% of the city, completely submerging some of its parishes. In some cases, only the tops of road signs showed above the water to indicate where homes had once been.

Before Katrina, Andrew was one of the most destructive storms ever recorded along the east coast, destroying more than 63 000 homes, causing $20 billion in property damage, and killing 27 people. Compared to Andrew, Hurricane Katrina has definitely caused more damage and claimed more lives. At its worst, wind speeds were as great as 235 kilometres per hour. It was the third most intense storm to strike the United States when it moved from Lake Pontchartrain to Louisiana.

Hurricane Katrina was formed over the Bahamas and made its first landfall in the southeastern coast of Florida. Originally considered a class one hurricane, it caused major flooding and loss of power, and killed eleven people. As it moved offshore, it weakened to the point where it was no longer thought to be a hurricane. However, it picked up force once it crossed the Gulf of Mexico. Meteorologists were surprised by how quickly it had regained wind speed. Katrina became a very wide hurricane spanning more than 320 km, building a water surge that rose to six metres around New Orleans.

Keywords

Identifying the **keywords** in a sentence or paragraph helps us remember the information better; it can be a study tool. For example, in "The destruction left by Katrina was insurmountable", the keywords are "Katrina", "destruction", and "insurmountable".

A. Underline the keywords in the following passage excerpts.

1. Flood waters covered 80% of the city, completely submerging some of its parishes.

2. Before Katrina, Andrew was one of the most destructive storms ever recorded along the east coast, destroying 63 000 homes, causing $20 billion in property damage, and killing 27 people.

3. Katrina became a very wide hurricane spanning more than 320 km, building a water surge that rose to six metres around New Orleans.

B. Write down five compound words from the passage and identify them as a noun, a verb, an adjective, or an adverb.

Did You Know?

Before Hurricane Katrina, New Orleans was famous for its Mardi Gras – "Fat Tuesday" – a French festival filled with food and drinks, parades, and street dancing.

Day
86
The Factual Composition (2)

Writing the Factual Composition

Steps:

1. Begin your writing with an opening paragraph. Write an interesting topic sentence to introduce your subject.

2. Compose interesting sentences from the group of facts. Vary the length and structure of each sentence to add variety. Add your own descriptive words.

3. Expand on the facts by adding examples or detailed descriptions.

4. Write a concluding paragraph to summarize your topic or give the reader something further to think about.

Make use of the facts about the Giant Squid in "The Factual Composition (1)" to write a factual composition.

Working title: _____

Opening paragraph:

_____

_____

_____

Body paragraphs:

1. _____

_____

_____

_____

2. _____

_____

_____

_____

3. _____

_____

_____

_____

Concluding paragraph:

_____

_____

_____

Follow these steps to complete your final copy.

Step One   **Edit and Proofread**

Read over your writing and look for errors in spelling and grammar. Make sure each sentence is complete with subject and verb. Make changes by adding, removing, or changing words.

Step Two   **Arrange Sentences**

Arrange the sentences you have composed into logical sequence so that you can get your ideas across in the best way.

Step Three   **Topic and Concluding Sentences**

See if your topic sentence clearly states your topic and arouses the reader's interest. Check your concluding sentence to make sure that it summarizes your ideas or provides an interesting after-thought to your topic.

Canada's Own Hurricane Alley

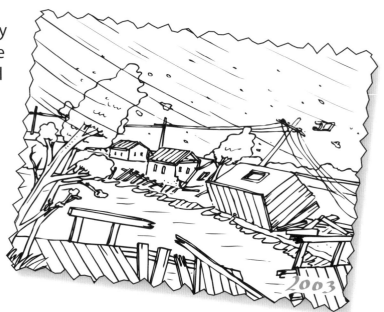

2003

Canadians do not seem to worry about tropical storms. But maybe they ought to. Since 1900, tropical storms have killed close to 895 people in Canada. Between 1950 and 2000, there were as many hurricanes off the country's east coast as there were off the United States' Hurricane Alley – the southern states stretching up from Florida.

Once in the Canadian region, the colder weather and water temperatures usually cause the winds of the storm to die down. Hurricanes need ocean temperatures of greater than 26.5°C to get the energy they need. Most hurricanes occur in September, when the oceans have had a long summer of heat. Once warm oceans meet the air above, swirling winds occur.

Canada's own "Hurricane Alley" is situated along the coasts of the Atlantic provinces: Nova Scotia, New Brunswick, Prince Edward Island, and Newfoundland.

Hurricane Juan pounded Nova Scotia in 2003. Environment Canada, on behalf of Nova Scotians and Prince Edward Islanders, requested that the name Juan be retired because of the lost lives and widespread destruction of trees across the two provinces. This was the first time that Canada had requested the retirement of a storm name.

If you are from Toronto, your grandparents might talk about Hurricane Hazel which hit in 1954. The city was flooded, and homes, roads, and bridges were destroyed. People were swept into rivers and drowned. On the night of October 18, Hurricane Hazel pelted Toronto with rain. Many people died from the flooding. The death toll reached 81.

What should you do if you hear that a hurricane is headed your way? Evacuate if ordered to do so. If the house is out of danger and well-built, stay at home, but make sure people and pets are inside. If you live near a body of water and the basement might flood, move everything in there to a higher floor. Remember that you should store drinking water, buy food that does not need refrigeration or cooking, check flashlights and battery-operated equipment, and make sure there is enough gasoline in the car. Also make sure you have cash on hand since the banks may not be open immediately after a hurricane!

Paraphrasing is a way of internalizing what we read. When we paraphrase a piece of writing, we rewrite it in our own words with the help of keywords.

A. Paraphrase each of the following passage excerpts.

1. Between 1950 and 2000, there were as many hurricanes off the country's east coast as there were off the United States' Hurricane Alley – the southern states stretching up from Florida.

_____

_____

2. Hurricanes need ocean temperatures of greater than 26.5°C to get the energy they need. Most hurricanes occur in September, when the oceans have had a long summer of heat. Once warm oceans meet the air above, swirling winds occur.

_____

_____

3. On the night of October 18, Hurricane Hazel pelted Toronto with rain. Many people died from the flooding. The death toll reached 81.

_____

_____

B. Answer the following questions.

1. Why should Canadians worry about tropical storms?

_____

_____

2. Where is Canada's "Hurricane Alley"?

_____

3. Why was the hurricane name "Juan" taken off the list?

_____

The Explanatory Composition

We write an **explanatory composition** to explain how to do something or how something works.

The planning:

– List the points to explain in logical order.

– Create an introduction that states the subject of your composition and arouses the reader's interest in reading your explanation.

– Include a concluding paragraph that sums up the explanation or asks the reader to think further about the topic.

A. Choose one of the following topics. Create an outline for your explanatory composition.

Organizing a Birthday Party

Planning for a Day Trip

Choosing a Pet

Topic: _____

Introductory idea: _____
_____

Points to explain: _____
_____
_____
_____
_____

Conclusion: _____
_____

Paragraphs in an Explanatory Composition

Introductory paragraph: This sets up your composition. You may want to mention what it is you are explaining, and how important or useful it is to know this information.

Body paragraphs: They contain step-by-step details of your explanation.

Concluding paragraph: This is a summary of your explanation or it can serve to provoke further thoughts.

B. **Based on your outline, write a finished copy of your explanatory composition.**

Title: _____

Introduction: _____

_____

_____

Body paragraphs: _____

_____

_____

_____

_____

_____

_____

_____

_____

_____

Concluding paragraph: _____

_____

_____

The Narrative Composition

We write a **narrative composition** to tell a story, true or imagined. It may be told in either the first person (using "I" or "we") or the third person (using "he", "she", "it", or "they").

The planning:

– Think of a general storyline.

– Set the time and place for your story.

– List the events in your story in the order in which they happen.

– Include a concluding paragraph that wraps up your story or leads the reader to think more about it.

A. **Choose one of the following topics or use a topic of your own. Create an outline for your narrative composition.**

To generate ideas, ask yourself the "Wh-" questions.

A Day at the CNE
Home Alone
A Day in the Life of a...

Topic: _____

General storyline: _____

_____

Time and place: _____

Events: _____

_____

_____

_____

Conclusion: _____

Paragraphs in a Narrative Composition

Introductory paragraph: This sets up your story. It usually includes the time and place.

Body paragraphs: They contain details of the events.

Concluding paragraph: This ends your story.

B. **Based on your outline, write a finished copy of your story.**

Title: _____

Introduction: _____

_____

Body paragraphs: _____

_____

_____

_____

_____

_____

_____

_____

_____

_____

_____

Concluding paragraph: _____

_____

_____

_____

Day 90

You Deserve A Break!

Read the clues and complete the crossword puzzle on weather.

Across

A. the degree of hotness or coldness of the environment

B. amount of moisture in the air

C. with strong and sudden rushes of wind

D. the changing of vapour into liquid

E. the changing of liquid into vapour

Down

1. any form of water that falls to the Earth's surface

2. a mixture of rain and snow

3. a violent storm of thunder, lightning, and heavy rain

4. covered with clouds

5. a severe tropical cyclone

6. hard, little ice balls that fall from the sky

7. also known as a "twister"

1 Get up!

A. 1. A pre-teen needs between eight and nine hours of sleep each night.
2. REMs are "rapid eye movements".
3. Phases three, four, and five are the most important.
4. (Suggested answer)
   lack of sleep
5. They might still be in deep sleep or REM sleep.

B. 1. woke
2. did ; done
3. had
4. chose
5. rode
6. paid
7. forgot
8. hidden

2 Grammar Overview (1)

A. 1. restaurant ; food
2. Beauty ; eye ; beholder
3. house ; storm
4. teacher ; poem ; friendship
5. place
6. end ; sense ; emptiness

B. 1. What
2. he
3. he
4. they
5. him
6. He
7. himself
8. it
9. she
10. their

C. The fox (has) excellent speed and can (reach) up to 50 km per hour. This speed, (coupled) with its cunning nature, has (made) the fox the traditional prey of the English foxhunt. Foxes often (retrace) their steps to throw off the scent of the pursuing hounds. They then (hide) in trees as the hounds and hunters (speed) past. Although foxes generally (stay) clear of humans, it (is) advisable not to approach them.

D. 1. difficult
2. national
3. frigid
4. British
5. frozen
6. silver
7. amateur

3 Video Games

A. 1. Fly a helicopter around the country to find and count the number of hungry people.
2. Plan a balanced diet for the people on a very small budget.
3. Plan the exact timing of the food drops from the helicopter, taking into account the wind direction.
4. Locate and order food from around the world while keeping costs down.
5. Transport the food by truck into Sheylan.
6. Help the community rebuild and become independent.

B. (Individual writing)

4 Grammar Overview (2)

A. 1. That performance was exceptionally good.
2. It has been almost a year since we last saw him. / It has almost been a year since we last saw him.
3. He was not good at that and did it rather oddly.
4. The slope was steep and they had to go down cautiously.
5. He nodded knowingly and started figuring out how to settle the matter.

B. 1. of
2. from
3. to
4. on
5. beyond
6. with
7. for
8. to
9. about

C. 1. although ; and
2. since / as / because
3. unless
4. but
5. since / as / because
6. if / when
7. or ; but

D. 1. Hey
2. Wow
3. Great
4. Oh no
5. Hurray
6. Look out
7. Yuck
8. Oops

5 Watch Where You Are Walking

A. A. PEDOMETER
B. TRANSMITS
C. INVENTION
D. PEDIATRIC
E. INSOLE
1. PREDICTS
2. DEVICE
3. PROTOTYPE

B. (Individual writing)

6 Verbs

A. 1. will go
2. was ; had expected
3. have not seen ; has been
4. dashed ; had sped

B. 1. The ripe apples were picked by the children.
2. The careless driver was warned by the police officer.
3. Sue borrowed the books for the project.
4. The second baseman caught the ball.
5. The classroom will be decorated for the party by us.
6. The puppy was left in the backyard by Della.

C. 1. IN
2. IN
3. IM
4. IN
5. IN
6. SUB

7 The Golden Arches

A. 1. Someone from San Bernardino had ordered a lot of malted milk mixing machines from him.
2. The food was ready before you ordered it.
3. He was able to open different locations of McDonald's and sell its products.
4. (Individual answer)

B. 1. earnings
2. hassle
3. zipped
4. amazed
5. expand
6. chain
7. franchise

8 The Subjunctive Mood

A. 1. If I were a billionaire, I would give you a million dollars.
2. Her parents demanded that she pay for the repair.

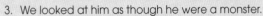

3. We looked at him as though he were a monster.
4. How I wish Jane were here with us.
5. If I were you, I would accept the offer right away.
6. The committee proposed that Mr. Sharma take up the position of CEO.
7. If Sam were the organizer, the show would be much better.
8. If she were to leave a month earlier, she would reach her destination on time.
9. The principal suggests that Matt read more but I wonder if Matt would heed the principal's advice.

B. (Suggested writing)
1. Valerie's mother suggested that she leave her project until the next day.
2. The doctor advises Mr. Sherwood that he get up earlier and exercise for half an hour before going to work.
3. The teacher demanded that Jeremy apologize to Patricia for his rudeness.
4. At the party, Janet socialized with everyone that came her way as if she were the hostess.

9 The Power of One

A. A. UPLIFTED   B. MARATHON
   C. ARTIFICIAL   D. DREAM
   1. ATHLETE   2. EXHAUSTED
   3. RESEARCH   4. AMPUTATED
B. 1. (Individual answer)
   2. He reached Thunder Bay, Ontario.
   3. (Individual answer)
   4. (Individual answer)

10 You Deserve A Break!

A. (Suggested answers)
1. telegram	2. thermostat
3. steal	4. treasure
5. thread	6. therapy
7. steak	8. teapot
9. steward	10. steady
11. theatre	12. tear
13. tolerate	14. teenage
15. treat	16. steam

B. (Colour these words.)
tree ; knee ; bee ; free ; me ; pea ; agree ; key ; flea ; sea ; we ; three

11 Verbals

A.
1. <u>to become</u> ; I	2. <u>swimming</u> ; G
3. <u>cooling</u> ; P	4. <u>laughing</u> ; P
5. <u>to see</u> ; I	6. <u>To settle</u> ; I
7. <u>jogging</u> ; G	8. <u>crossing</u> ; P
9. <u>climbing</u> ; P	10. <u>cooking</u> ; G
11. <u>to leave</u> ; I	12. <u>driving</u> ; G

B. (Individual writing)

12 Levi Strauss and the Old Blue Jeans

A. 1. B   2. C   3. C   4. C
B. (Individual drawing and writing)

13 Verbal Phrases

A. 1. a skiing trip
   2. Skiing downhill
   3. to keep my balance
   4. tobogganing more than skiing
   5. taking a rest
   6. the skiing pants
   7. Drinking a cup of hot chocolate ; the first skiing lesson
   8. sitting on the snow
   9. buried deep in the snow
   10. a torn mitten
B. 1. N   2. N   3. ADV
   4. ADJ   5. ADV
C. (Individual writing)

14 The McIntosh Apple

A. 1. F   2. T   3. T
   4. T   5. F   6. T
B. A. TRANSPLANTED   B. FOCUSED
   C. DISMAY   D. SCIONS
   1. TECHNIQUES   2. FARMHAND
   3. PIONEERS

15 Some Vexing Agreements

A. 1. likes   2. One   3. is
   4. knows   5. All   6. spells
   7. are   8. was   9. practises
   10. have   11. are   12. One
B. 1. Either you or I am eligible for the scholarship.
   3. The coach, as well as the players, was very disappointed with the decision.
   4. Each of the children was given a basket of strawberries.
   6. Neither the class nor the teacher has heard of the news.
   7. None of the committee members was prepared to vote.
   8. Has any one of you met our new principal before?
   10. None of the houses has been damaged.
   11. Someone holding three parcels at the door wants to talk to you.
   12. Everyone attending the wedding ceremony was happy for them.

16 The CN Tower – the World's Tallest Structure

A. Facts:
(Any five of these)
– the world's tallest freestanding structure
– cost $63 000 000 to build

- took 1500 workers to complete
- made of reinforced concrete
- 185 storeys or 533 metres high
- opened on June 26, 1976
- has two million visitors a year
- has four lookout levels
- has glass floor and outdoor Observation Deck
- restaurant offers 360-degree view of Toronto

Opinions:

(In any order)

1. one of Ontario's prime tourist attractions
2. will likely remain the world's tallest freestanding structure
3. will probably cost $300 000 000 to build today
4. an impressive building
5. the "Jewel of Toronto"

B. 1. Satellite broadcasting has replaced the need for tall broadcast towers.
   2. (Individual answer)
   3. (Individual answer)

17 Relative Pronouns and Interrogative Pronouns

A. 1. which   2. whom   3. that
   4. who   5. that   6. that

B. 1. The teacher likes the picture which Jamie drew.
   2. The teacher whom everyone admires is leaving us.
   3. We watched a film which was about the discovery of America.
   4. The young man who works part-time as a lifeguard is his brother.
   5. The dish which her mother cooked won the grand award.
   6. The tree which we planted last summer now stands taller than I.

C. 1. Who   2. Which   3. whom
   4. which   5. Whose   6. Who
   7. Which   8. whom

18 The Poppy – a Symbol for Remembrance Day

A. 1. It means place or location.
   2. No. Dandelions grow easily in Canada. If poppies fill the fields like dandelions, then it means they grow easily too.
   3. (Suggested answer)
      A "symbol" is an object that represents something significant.
   4. "Sacrifice" means "the loss of lives".

B. (Individual writing)

19 Commas

A. 1. The farmer gave us some carrots, a few apples, and a lot of potatoes.
   2. Of course, they won't let him join the game again.
   3. Indeed, it was the best we could do for her.
   4. The incident happened on June 19, 2004.
   5. Once we start, we should continue and not give up.
   6. Although I didn't see it happen, I could feel the horror.
   7. The little boy replied, "I just asked for some candies."
   8. Did you see the sleek, blue sports car on the driveway?
   9. Mrs. Thomson, our next door neighbour, told us not to worry.
   10. The storm left the village with flooded basements, fallen trees, and mudslides.

B. 1. Our dog, which everyone loves, likes eating snacks.
   4. On my way to school, I ran into Jim's mother, who told me that Jim was not feeling well.
   6. She let me see her camera, which was as thin as a credit card.
   11. Pam's younger sister, who looks very much like her, will come to the party too.
   12. Mrs. Steele, whose son is about my age, bakes great cookies.

20 You Deserve A Break!

1. tear   2. three
3. mate / meat / tame   4. earth
5. toast   6. dairy
7. crate / trace   8. sore
9. relay   10. scent
11. mane / mean   12. sue
13. form   14. dawn
15. cola   16. foal
17. care / race   18. hare
19. flee   20. grin

21 A Canadian Artist and a War Memorial

A. 1. She has a bowed head to symbolize mourning.
   2. They traditionally symbolize victory.
   3. It is to represent a sense of loss because the war took too many lives to achieve victory.

B. (Individual writing)

22 More on Commas

A. (Suggested writing)
   1. It was a truly memorable event. Everyone had a good time.
   2. The game went down to the bottom of the ninth inning but we didn't lose hope.
   3. I answered the door and an old man handed me a parcel.
   4. When they went in, they saw a man in his late 30s. He was dressing the wound in his leg.
   5. Since the road was slippery, the truck slid into a ditch. Luckily, the driver was not hurt.
   6. I put the book on the top shelf but someone must have taken it away.
   7. After knowing that we will soon face the toughest team, the coach wants us to practise more. Only then can we stand a chance of winning.

8. If they began earlier, they might be able to finish it, but there is simply not enough time now.

B. (Suggested writing)

In his first season of organized hockey, Gretzky managed to score just one goal. However, in his second season, he scored 27, and 104 in his third season. By the time Wayne was ten, he scored an astounding 378 goals in a single season.

Wayne's idol was Gordie Howe who was with the Detroit Red Wings and held numerous scoring titles. Little did Wayne know that he would go on to break all of his idol's records and set new ones that seem insurmountable even today.

23 What's Your Point of View?

A. (Individual writing)
B. (Individual writing)

24 Colons and Semicolons

A.
1. The chairman neglected one crucial fact: the report was not ready.
2. We all have the same goal: win the tournament this time.
3. The old saying goes: "Blood is thicker than water."
4. They were told to pack these for the trip: a flashlight, a compass, and a radio.
5. The company had the following openings: secretary, receptionist, administrative assistant.
6. The article "Travel in Asia: China and India" is an interesting read.
7. We expect only one thing from him: complete the project by next Monday.
8. Do remember this: never ever give up.
9. He came up with a brilliant idea: combine the two into one.
10. The instructor told us to get ready these items: a glove, a bat, a helmet, and a few baseballs.

B. (Individual writing)

C.
1. To prepare himself for the race, he performed the following exercises every day: weightlifting, which built his upper body strength; running, which built up his endurance; biking, which strengthened his leg muscles.
2. They met with John; it was a brief meeting.
3. He was introduced to the following people: Jason, Peter's cousin; Mandy, his boss's daughter; Sam, the secretary's husband.
4. It was chilly out there; the temperature dropped to a mere 2°C.
5. We tried our best to finish it on time; however, we couldn't make it.
6. She's such a popular athlete; wherever she goes, she's surrounded by fans.
7. He found himself face to face with someone he knew; it was Corey.
8. The surprise gift finally arrived; it was a nifty DVD player.

9. No one wanted to leave; they were all eager for the announcement.
10. We had a sumptuous dinner; everyone was full.

D. (Individual writing)

25 The Black Loyalists

A. (Individual writing)
B. (Individual writing)

26 Dashes and Hyphens

A.
1. The final showdown – the do-or-die game – will be telecast live.
2. Everything boiled down to one word – perseverance.
3. The Greatest Game Ever Played – the story of an underdog golfer – is the best motivational film I have ever watched.
4. No matter what you do – explaining, pleading, or begging – won't make her change her mind.
5. Digital cameras, cell phones, and MP3 players – these are gadgets we almost can't do without.

B.
1. The new manager is a twenty-three-year-old graduate.
2. This is a once-in-a-lifetime chance that you shouldn't miss.
3. Non-members are not allowed to go in the members-only lounge.
4. The semi-final for the above eighteen contestants will start next week.
5. He lives in a twenty-five-year-old split-level bungalow.
6. A lot of people were inspired by his from-rags-to-riches story.
7. The report shows that two-thirds of the population are under fifty-five years of age.
8. The pro-government rally was held a block away from the anti-government protest.

27 The Ghost of Cherry Hill House

A. Fact:
– carpenters and labourers found previously locked-up tools scattered on the attic floor
– managers have reported seeing a woman in a white dress in the attic if they stayed past midnight
Opinion:
(Individual writing)

B. (Individual writing)

28 More Punctuation Devices

A.
1. The new museum (see inset) will be officially opened on August 21, 2007.
2. The honour students (of which I am one) are invited to the ceremony.
3. The complimentary tickets (a pair from Uncle Charlie and another pair from Mr. Todd) came just in time.
4. They should (a) get a form (b) fill it out (c) get their parents' consent and (d) return it to their teacher before noon tomorrow.

5. The merger (yet to be confirmed) is said to take effect in January 2007.
6. The graph (Fig. 2b) shows the population growth over the past 20 years.
7. The series (2-2) would be decided in the final game to be played this afternoon.
8. The supporting role (Captain Truman) was given to a little-known actor by the name of Willie Whitt.

B.
1. Recent research indicates that most of the asteroids orbit around...the chance that an asteroid strikes the Earth is one in a million.
2. Malls sprout up in big cities due to...the largest shopping centre in the world is the West Edmonton Mall in Edmonton.
3. Malawi is an impoverished third world country in Africa. The infant mortality rate...the average life expectancy is only 37 years.
4. There are many ways to conserve energy...with more and more people switch to driving smaller cars which are more fuel-efficient.
5. Roberta Bondar became the first female astronaut to go into space. She received the Order of Canada...In 1998, Roberta was named to the Canadian Medical Hall of Fame.
6. The cell phone has become almost an indispensable gadget...the government is beginning to look into regulating the use of the cell phone.
7. A Great White ranges from five to seven metres in length and weighs...swimming at a speed of 16 to 20 km per hour, the Great White usually attacks its prey from behind or beneath.

29 The Titanic

A. (Underline these sentences.)
1. Launched on April 10, 1912, this luxurious ocean liner left the British port of Southampton with 2227 people aboard.
2. (Same as 1.)
3. It also carried the mummified body of an ancient Egyptian princess who had been a member of the Cult of the Dead during Egyptian times.
4. (Same as 3.)
5. Did the mummified princess bring a curse on the voyage of the Titanic?
6. The Titanic collided with an enormous iceberg just moments after the iceberg was sighted at 11:40 p.m. on April 14, 1912.
7. This mammoth ship, that was supposed to be so safe, sank completely and rapidly and led to the deaths of 1522 people.

(Suggested writing)
1. very expensive and comfortable
2. set sail
3. preserved
4. of a very long time ago
5. evil spell
6. huge
7. huge like the large extinct elephant

B. (Individual writing)

30 You Deserve A Break!

A.

B.
1. space shuttle
2. Venus
3. Pluto
4. universe
5. Jupiter
6. Uranus
7. alien
8. Solar System
9. comet
10. astronaut

31 Cause and Effect

1. An oxygen tank of Apollo 13 exploded and the spacecraft failed to navigate.
2. The number of whales in Johnstone Strait peaks during this period.
3. We have pairs of chromosomes that represent the combined contribution of our father and mother.
4. a. The plates split and this leads to earthquakes.
   b. An earthquake in Portugal killed many people and ruined the city of Lisbon.

32 Sasquatch – Canada's Legendary Monster

A.
1. T   2. T   3. T
4. F   5. T   6. F
7. F   8. T

B.
1. The Sasquatch could only survive by hiding in the day and coming out at night.
2. (Individual answer)
3. (Individual answer)

33 Framing Questions

(Individual writing)

34 Canada's Youngest Territory

Meaning: "our land"
Established: April 1, 1999
Main population group: Inuit

Official languages: Inuktitut, Dene, English, French
Location: next to the Northwest Territories
Size: twice the size of British Columbia / largest of all provinces and territories
Art: soapstone carvings
Activities: seal fishing, dog sledding
Unique feature: consensus government – equal number of male and female legislative members

35 Direct and Indirect Speech (1)

A.
1. Ivan says that he always enjoys window-shopping with them.
2. Mr. Ross said that they had been working on the project.
3. Fred's father said that he would attend the ceremony.
4. Karen said that she was never good at singing.
5. Ted explained that the moon revolves around the Earth.
6. Evelyn told Mrs. Wayne that they had tried many ways.
7. Mabel said that she liked the cotton dress more.

B.
1. Alex told his father that he had not played in the game the day before.
2. Ron said that it had happened a week before.
3. Molly said that her grandma would come two days later.
4. The waiter said that they served fresh seafood that day.
5. The teacher said that the following week, there would be two new students in their class.
6. Bill said that they had gone to Hamilton the week before.

36 Could You Pass a Citizenship Test?

1. English and French
2. (Answer will vary through the years.)
3. John A. Macdonald
4. Ottawa
5. 1867
6. ten provinces and three territories
7. the First Nations, the Inuit, and the Métis
8. Lake Huron, Lake Ontario, Lake Michigan, Lake Erie, and Lake Superior

37 Direct and Indirect Speech (2)

A. (Suggested writing)
1. Mrs. Watson asked Ben which was the one he wanted.
2. They asked when they could start.
3. The police officer asked if I had come that way.
4. She asked him if he was going with her the following day.
5. Mrs. Healey asked her neighbour whether he/she had seen her cat.

B. (Suggested writing)
1. Margaret said to me, "I want to buy this bracelet."
2. "There will not be any games until next Saturday," the coach said to the players.
3. The teacher said, "It is a holiday tomorrow."
4. "Can you take me to your school?" the woman asked them.
5. Carol asked Bill, "Have you got an MP3 player?"
6. "Is there anyone in the house?" the delivery man asked.

C.
1. The man said that he would let me know the following week.
2. I asked him if he had seen my Science book.
3. The librarian asked if I had borrowed the storybook.
4. I remarked that there are 29 days in February every four years.
5. Wendy said that she had lived there for almost 10 years.

D. Felix said that they would have a game with Harry's team the following day but they had not quite prepared yet because a lot of his teammates were still busy with their projects and they did not have time for practice. He thought they would lose.

38 The Mohawk Poet

1. (Individual writing)
2. (Individual writing)
3. rains, chains, plains ;
wanes, rains, plains

39 Phrases

A.
1. the fluffy, creepy thing
2. The losing team ; a good fight ; the end
3. the long, uphill climb
4. a cool, refreshing drink ; the pool
5. an extremely boring movie
6. seven honour students ; our class
7. a delicious cheesecake
8. The red, sleek sports car ; an arrow
9. a warm and fun reception
10. No one ; that thick, oily substance
11. The long, bumpy ride ; an hour
12. the most skilful player

B.
1. (across the ditch)
2. in the cooler
3. (in the hallway)
4. of the team
5. (That afternoon) ; (in the compound)
6. from his group
7. (through the tunnel)
8. of the opposing team
9. (from morning to night)
10. (up the tall tree)
11. (all over the place)
12. of the palace

C. (Individual writing)

40 You Deserve A Break!

A. SCALLOP   B. SPAGHETTI
C. SNAKE   D. SNAIL
E. SMELL   F. STICK
1. SKUNK   2. SMART
3. SLITHER   4. STAMPEDE
5. SLOW   6. SMOOTH
7. SCORPION

41 Beothuks – Newfoundland's Native People

A.   A. TUBERCULOSIS   B. SCAVENGE
     C. FURRIERS   D. TRAPPERS
     1. ABDUCTED   2. CAPTIVE
     3. BAND   4. ABORIGINAL
B.   (Suggested writing)
     Paragraph 1:
     One reason for the extinction of the Beothuks is that they moved away from sources of food in order to avoid European contact.
     Paragraph 2:
     The Beothuks were reduced to a refugee population by the 19th century as the English settlement expanded in Newfoundland.
     Paragraph 3:
     One of the last known Beothuk women was abducted by the English settlers in St. John's and renamed Mary March.
     Paragraph 4:
     The wife of the governor of Newfoundland seemed fascinated by the Beothuk woman but did not seem to care that she would miss her child.

42 Adjective and Adverb Phrases

A.   1. in the pool ; adv
     2. for storing stationery and books ; adv
     3. on the bench ; adj
     4. with a huge pink bow ; adj
     5. on the table ; adj
     6. on weekends ; adv
     7. with a long tail ; adj
     8. from the daycare centre ; adj
     9. into the hole ; adv
     10. in the morning ; adv
B.   (Individual writing)
C.   (Individual writing)

43 UNESCO

A.   (Suggested answers)
     1. tradition   2. protect
     3. special / distinct   4. preservation
     5. idea   6. universal
     7. help   8. cannot be replaced
B.   (Suggested answers)
     1. culturally important
     2. historically important
     3. geologically important
     4. biologically diverse / unique
     5. the only site of its kind
C.   (Individual writing)

44 Clauses

A.   1. IND   2. IND   3. D   4. D
     5. IND   6. D   7. IND   8. IND
     9. D   10. IND   11. D   12. IND
B.   (Individual writing)
C.   (Individual writing)

45 Head Smashed-in Buffalo Jump

A.   (Individual writing)
B.   (Suggested writing)
     Food: marrow ; meat
     Clothing: hair ; hide
     Tools: horns ; bones ; hide ; hooves
     Ceremonial Objects: tail ; hooves ; skull
     (Individual answer)

46 Compound and Complex Sentences

A.   (Individual writing)
B.   (Individual writing)
C.   1. CCX   2. C   3. CX
     4. CX   5. C
D.   (Suggested writing)
     1. Since everyone was tired, no one wanted to continue.
     2. Katie went to the dentist because she had a toothache.
     3. I was walking to school when I met the old man and his dog.

47 L'Anse aux Meadows – a UNESCO World Heritage Site

A.   (Suggested writing)
     Exploration
     – Lief Eriksson with a crew of 30
     – vessel with a square sail
     – travelled from Greenland
     Settlement
     – grass-covered buildings
     – houses, workshops, and small forge
     – near a peat bog
     – duration unknown
     Discovery
     – found in 1960 by archaeologists
     UNESCO Site
     – excavated for eight years
     – three Norse buildings and a vessel recreated
     – declared UNESCO site in 1978
     – guides stay in character
B.   (Individual writing)

48 Building Vocabulary

A. 1. unable ; ability
    2. tolerable / tolerant ; tolerance
    3. quicken ; quickly
    4. infertile ; fertility
    5. informal ; formality
    6. unsuccessful ; success

B. 1. discover   2. seem   3. divide
    4. probable   5. monument   6. adventure
    7. act   8. ordinary   9. satisfy
    10. sport

C. 1. hyperactive   2. outsmart
    3. anti-government   4. miscalculate
    5. predawn   6. impossible
    7. misunderstand   8. dissatisfied
    9. submerged   10. unfit
    (Suggested answers)
    11. helpful ; helpless ; helpfulness ; helplessly ; helper
    12. truth ; truthful ; truthfully ; truthfulness ; truly

49 Rock My World!

A. 1. D   2. E   3. A
    4. B   5. C

B. 1. (Individual answer)
    2. There are fjords, seacoast, forests, and mountains.
    3. It is the site of the oldest rocks in Canada.

50 You Deserve A Break!

    1. Jack and the Beanstalk
    2. The Emperor's New Suit
    3. Goldilocks and the Three Bears
    4. The Wizard of Oz
    5. Charlie and the Chocolate Factory
    6. Little Red Riding Hood
    7. Hansel and Gretel
    8. The Little Match-Seller
    9. Beauty and the Beast
    10. Alice in Wonderland
    (Individual drawing of the book covers)

51 Homophone Challenge

A. 1. sale   2. brake   3. theirs
    4. mussels   5. stares   6. hear
    7. pour   8. whether

B. 1. paws ; pause   2. suede ; swayed
    3. read ; red   4. scent ; cent
    5. jeans ; genes   6. Sunday ; sundae
    7. bear ; bare

C. A. BOUGH   B. PRINCIPAL
    C. FEAT   D. RAYS
    1. WAIST   2. SUITES
    3. BOARDER   4. VARY

52 The First Maps

    1. (Individual drawing)

    2. (Individual answer)
    3. (Individual answer)
Challenge
(Individual writing)

53 Synonyms and Antonyms

A. (Suggested answers)
    1. fervent   2. accurate   3. happy
    4. brisk   5. serious   6. sensitive
    7. prediction ; convalesce
    8. studied ; sample ; categorization
    9. huge ; slept

B. 1. A. BULKY   B. SMOOTH
        Down: LOSS
    2. A. OUTSKIRT   B. DEPRESSED
        Down: OCCUPIED
    3. A. BRISK   B. CLEAR
        Down: RARE
    4. A. SWIFT   B. INTELLIGENT
        Down: FINAL

54 Marco Polo – a Medieval Explorer

A. 1. F   2. F   3. T   4. T
    5. F   6. F   7. F   8. T

B. 1. E   2. C   3. D   4. F
    5. A   6. B
Challenge
(Individual writing)

55 Mixing up Words

A. 1. a. except   b. accept
    2. a. advise   b. advice
    3. a. imminent   b. eminent
    4. a. childlike   b. childish
    5. a. respectful   b. respectable

B. 1. Could   2. besides   3. sensible
    4. eagerly   5. As   6. theft

C. (Individual writing)

56 Racing to the Finish Line?

    1. The main character suddenly stumbles, instead of sprinting to the finish line as expected.
    2. (Suggested answer)
       It is there to indicate doubt.
    3. (Individual answer)
    4. (Individual writing)

57 Tricky Usage

    1. a. Among   b. between   c. among
    2. a. each other b. one another   c. each other
    3. a. fewer   b. less   c. less
    4. a. Lie   b. lay   c. lie
    5. a. into   b. into   c. in
    6. a. sit   b. set   c. sit
    7. a. it's   b. its   c. its

58 Mars

A. 1. It takes Mars almost two years to orbit around the sun.
2. There may be water on Mars; if not, it is at least capable of sustaining water.
3. (Suggested answer)
They themselves are not yet capable of travelling to Mars with the existing technology.
4. There may be water on Mars to sustain life in the future.

B. A. GALAXY   B. EVIDENCE
   C. ORBIT   D. AXIS
   1. ACTIVE   2. VOLCANOES
   3. SPIN

59 Frequently Confused Words

A. 1. presents   2. than
3. patients   4. principal
5. It's   6. fourth
7. theirs   8. through
9. waste   10. fares
11. accept   12. sight
13. stationary   14. conscious
15. past

B. 1. effect ; affect   2. miner ; minor
3. advice ; advise   4. quiet ; quite
5. all ready ; already

C. (Individual writing)

60 You Deserve A Break!

A. 1. wafer   2. bar   3. fudge
4. brownie   5. sundae   6. cake
7. fondue   8. mousse   9. pastry
10. parfait   11. truffle   12. popsicle

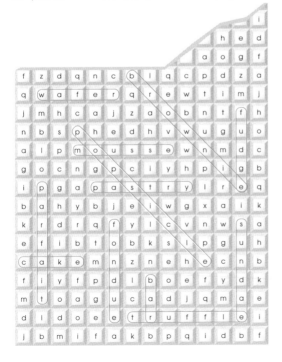

61 How Many Are There?

1. Scientists may use size, shape, and colour.
2. (Any three of these)
the jungle cat, the black-footed cat, the cheetah, the Canadian lynx
3. The word is "warm-blooded".
4. They give birth to live young, breathe air, and feed their young milk from mammary glands.
5. (Suggested answer)
We can then better understand the world around us.

Challenge
(Individual writing)

62 Faulty Sentence Construction

A. (Suggested writing)
1. My sister always wants to get the lead role and become famous.
2. Weight gain is often the result of eating too much candy and junk food, and eating between meals.
3. It is important to work hard and do well in school.
4. They think science projects are more interesting than English projects.
5. Her success was due to her perseverance, hard work, and the support from her family.

B. (Suggested writing)
1. They baked a specially huge birthday cake for her.
2. Posing as a tourist, the undercover police officer caught the pickpocket.
3. My father earned almost three thousand dollars more for the additional work.
4. She read with her sister the story about Little Ann.
5. Talking to his mother, he caught sight of a spider.

63 Bears

A. Polar
Physical Appearance:
– thick white fur
Characteristics:
– layer of insulating fat
– greatest hunter of all bears
– can swim 100 km without rest
Black
Physical Appearance:
– about 136 kg
– averages 1.8 m long
Characteristics:
– hibernates throughout winter
Grizzly
Physical Appearance:
– up to 450 kg
Characteristics:
– hibernates throughout winter
Kodiak
Physical Appearance:
– 2.75 m tall
– up to 725 kg

Characteristics:
- eats plants and roots
- loves salmon
- largest of all bears
Honey
Physical Appearance:
- 1.2 m long
- 45 kg
Characteristics:
- smallest of all bears

B. 1. (Individual answer)
    2. The fish get contaminated in polluted waters.
    3. They can use the information to suggest ways of protecting bear populations.

64 Writing Interesting Sentences

A. (Suggested writing)
    1. Over the plain a crimson sun set.
    2. In the locker room assembled the players for a pep talk.
    3. Fish and chips was what she wanted to eat.
    4. To avoid the tag, he moved deftly to the side.
    5. To save her from the flood, the firefighters raced against time.
    6. Through the narrow alley sped the motorbike.
    7. With two out and one on third base, he scored the winning run.
    8. In the breeze flew gracefully the kites.
B. (Individual writing)
C. (Individual writing)

65 Hidden Depths

A. 1. biology   2. marine
    3. fascination   4. NASA
    5. oceanographers   6. Halifax
    7. venture   8. behemoth
B. 1. They were the United States, Canada, Russia, and China.
    2. The project involved exploring unknown areas of the ocean, like NASA's exploration of space.
    3. They use specialized vehicles and life support systems.
    4. (Individual answer)

66 Concise Writing

A. (Suggested writing)
    1. The weather report called for sunny sky and mild temperature so Jason decided to go on a bike ride. He invited his friend Ron to join him.
    2. Ron rode a 12-speed bike which was a birthday present from his grandfather last year. Jason's was a 10-speed bike which was given by his brother and was like new.
    3. They rode for an hour and stopped for refreshment and some rest. Part of the ride was up a long slope. Since they were not used to riding uphill, they were very tired.

B. (Suggested writing)
    1. Because there was a severe snowstorm, many flights were delayed or cancelled and the passengers were waiting anxiously in the crowded airport.
    2. Paul was a responsible boy who delivered newspapers seven days a week, even in bad weather.
    3. Since the cave was pitch dark and eerie, the children held their breath and dared not make a sound.

67 Bear Attack

A. (Individual writing)
B. (Suggested writing)
    If you see a bear:
    - Keep a cool head.
    - Never try to outrun a bear.
    - Never remove your backpack.
    - Roll yourself into a tight ball if the bear is about to attack.
    (Individual design)

68 Similes and Metaphors

A. (Individual writing)
B. 1. the artery
    2. a bear
    3. the sunshine
    4. a prison
    5. a vulture's eye
C. (Individual writing)

69 Advice Column

(Individual writing)

70 You Deserve A Break!

A. MARATHON   B. SKATEBOARDING
C. BASEBALL   D. ARCHERY
E. KAYAKING   F. SKIING
1. BASKETBALL   2. SOCCER
3. BADMINTON   4. WINDSURFING
5. HOCKEY   6. GOLF

71 Add Colour to Your Writing

A. 1. cavernous   2. scampered
    3. considerate   4. ecstatic
    5. towering
B. 1. gentle   2. green
    3. towering   4. swaying
    5. leaning   6. swooped
    7. enjoy   8. cool
    9. refresh   10. peaceful
C. 1. We want to go to the park to have a game of baseball.
    2. I don't think it is proper to do that.
    3. I remember they broke the record two years ago.

4. She doesn't seem to realize the crux of the problem.
5. They were all eager to take part in it.
6. Since today is a public holiday, the malls are closed.
7. He saw the key in the lock.
8. I may be late if I don't hurry.

72 Sweden's Road Charge

A. (Suggested writing)
Paragraph 1:
To protect the air above our planet, many countries have signed the Kyoto Accord to reduce greenhouse gas emissions.
Paragraph 2:
Although Sweden is a leader in adhering to Kyoto's clean air program, traffic pollution is on the rise in Stockholm. This is why the city employs staff to monitor its traffic and make changes when necessary.
Paragraph 3:
To encourage car pooling and reduce congestion, Stockholm has been charging visitors a border crossing fee since January of 2006. Rush hour visitors are charged a higher rate.
Paragraph 4:
The road charge program will undergo an 18-month trial. In the meantime, the income from it will be used to improve public transit.

B. (Individual writing)

73 Imagery in Poetry

A. (Individual answers)
B. (Individual writing)
C. (Individual answers)
D. (Individual writing)

74 Bio-gas Fuelled Cars

A. 1. Pollution and gasoline prices are both on the rise.
2. Plants produce it from raw sewage sludge, household scraps, slaughterhouse waste, or food industry leftovers.
3. "With Sweden leading the way to a new alternative fuel, we can only wonder why other countries continue to drag their heels."
4. "By 2020, there could be over one million cars running on this alternative fuel system."

B. (Individual writing)

75 Acrostic Poems

A. (Individual answers)
B. (Individual writing)
C. (Individual writing)

76 Do Cell Phones Cause Accidents?

A. (Individual writing)
B. (Individual writing)

77 Troubleshooting Confusing Writing

A. (Suggested writing)
1. Andrew asked Peter to explain Peter's problem.
2. Janice told her best friend Mandy that Janice had won the first prize.
3. The girls in grade six competed against the boys and the boys lost.
4. Rob met Sam when Sam first joined the school team.
5. Matt argued with Paul and Matt was furious.
6. The father and the son did not know what to do so the father suggested putting it aside first.
7. The Jays and the Yankees each scored a run in the seventh inning, and the Jays were confident that they would tie the game soon.

B. (Suggested writing)
1. Walking to school, he saw Ashley's dog.
2. She spent almost all of her savings. Now she is poor.
3. After he was rescued, he told his family about his brush with death.
4. Mike being the youngest in the family, no one listens to him.
5. Laughing out loud, the children were entertained by the naughty monkey.
6. Last Sunday, he talked endlessly about his exciting trip.
7. Sailing down the river, the children spotted a big fish.

78 Timepieces

A. 1. Smart Personal Objects Technology
2. Microsoft Network
3. frequency modulation

B. 1. (Any two of these)
– allows you to access up-to-the-minute information like news and weather
– can be synchronized with the calendar on personal computer
– can send and receive messages
– uses wireless transmission available in many North American cities
2. It is available in 12 Canadian cities and 100 American cities.
3. A compass can also be added.
4. (Individual answer)
5. (Individual answer)
6. (Individual answer)

79 Writing Paragraphs

A. 1. 4 ; 2 ; 3 ; 1
2. 4 ; 3 ; 1 ; 2
3. 4 ; 1 ; 2 ; 3

B. (Individual writing)

80 You Deserve A Break!

Insect: beetle ; dragonfly ; earwig ; grasshopper ; housefly ; ladybug ; mosquito ; moth

Non-insect: centipede ; crab ; earthworm ; scorpion ; snail ; spider
(Individual colouring of the insects)

81 Holograms

A.

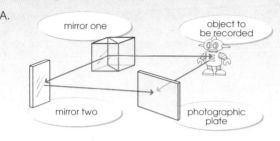

mirror one
object to be recorded
mirror two
photographic plate

B. 1. illuminate
    2. photographs / pictures
    3. refined
    4. counterfeit
    5. laser beam

82 Writing Ads

A. (Individual writing)
B. (Individual writing)

83 Facts about Hurricanes

1. over 155 km per hour ; over 5.5 m
2. 74 to 95 km per hour ; 1 to 1.5 m
3. category 3 ; extensive

Challenge
(Individual writing)

84 The Factual Composition (1)

The Giant Squid's physical appearance:
2 ; 6 ; 7 ; 8 ; 9 ; 10 ; 14 ; 15 ; 18
Living habits:
1 ; 3 ; 4 ; 12 ; 13
What we don't know about the Giant Squid:
5 ; 11 ; 16 ; 17 ; 19

85 The Destruction of New Orleans

A. 1. <u>Flood</u> waters covered <u>80% of the city</u>, completely <u>submerging</u> some of its <u>parishes</u>.
    2. <u>Before Katrina</u>, <u>Andrew</u> was one of the <u>most destructive</u> storms ever recorded along the <u>east coast</u>, destroying <u>more than 63 000 homes</u>, causing <u>$20 billion in property damage</u>, and killing <u>27 people</u>.
    3. <u>Katrina</u> became a very wide hurricane <u>spanning more than 320 km</u>, building a <u>water surge</u> that rose to <u>six metres</u> around <u>New Orleans</u>.
B. (In any order)
    rooftops ; noun
    overpasses ; noun
    landfall ; noun
    southeastern ; adjective
    offshore ; adverb

86 The Factual Composition (2)

(Individual writing)

87 Canada's Own Hurricane Alley

A. (Suggested writing)
    1. From 1950 to 2000, the number of hurricanes off Canada's east coast and off the United States' southern states was roughly the same.
    2. Hurricanes occur when the oceans have had a long summer of heat and become warmer than 26.5 °C. That is why most of them are in September.
    3. The death toll reached 81 when Hurricane Hazel flooded Toronto on October 18.
B. 1. Tropical storms have killed almost 895 people in Canada since 1900, and the number of hurricanes off the country's east coast and off the United States' Hurricane Alley has been the same.
    2. It is along the coasts of Nova Scotia, New Brunswick, Prince Edward Island, and Newfoundland.
    3. It did too much damage across Nova Scotia and Prince Edward Island.

88 The Explanatory Composition

A. (Individual writing)
B. (Individual writing)

89 The Narrative Composition

A. (Individual writing)
B. (Individual writing)

90 You Deserve A Break!

A. TEMPERATURE   B. HUMIDITY
C. GUSTY   D. CONDENSATION
E. EVAPORATION
1. PRECIPITATION   2. SLEET
3. THUNDERSTORM   4. OVERCAST
5. HURRICANE   6. HAIL
7. TORNADO